A Buddhist Grief Observed

A BUDDHIST GRIEF OBSERVED

GUY NEWLAND

Wisdom Publications
199 Elm Street
Somerville, MA 02144 USA
wisdompubs.org

© 2016 Guy Newland
All rights reserved.

Library of Congress Cataloging-in-Publication Data
Names: Newland, Guy, author.
Title: A Buddhist grief observed / by Guy Newland.
Description: Somerville : Wisdom Publications, 2016. | Includes
    bibliographical references.
Identifiers: LCCN 2015041176| ISBN 9781614293019 (pbk. : alk. paper) |
    ISBN 1614293015 (pbk. : alk. paper)
Subjects: LCSH: Death—Religious aspects—Buddhism. | Grief—Religious
    aspects—Buddhism. | Loss (Psychology)—Religious aspects—Buddhism.
Classification: LCC BQ4487 .N49 2016 | DDC 294.3/423—dc23
LC record available at https://lccn.loc.gov/2015041176

ISBN 978-1-61429-301-9   ebook ISBN 978-1-61429-322-4
20 19 18 17 16   5 4 3 2 1

Author photo is by Robert Barclay. Cover design by Philip Pascuzzo.
Interior design by Gopa&Ted2, Inc. Set in Weiss 10.75/15.

Wisdom Publications' books are printed on acid-free paper and meet
the guidelines for permanence and durability of the Production Guidelines for
Book Longevity of the Council on Library Resources.

❦ This book was produced with environmental mindfulness.
For more information, please visit wisdompubs.org/wisdom-environment.

Printed in the United States of America.

Please visit fscus.org.

For Gabe, Becca, and everyone else

It is nothing strange that humans beings
should die.

THE BUDDHA

Don't come talking to me about the
consolations of religion or I shall suspect
that you don't understand.

C. S. LEWIS

Contents

Introduction   1

Pain   5
Intimacy   15
The Great Matter   27
Karma   45
Taking Care   57

Eulogy   81
Resources   91
Acknowledgments   93
Notes   95
About the Author   115

Introduction

Grief is the process of adjusting to unwanted change, and since change is unrelenting, we bear every day unrecognized microgriefs. Call it stress: we just feel like a massage or, perhaps, we think we need a drink. Loss and fear of loss give us our daily shape as we feel and think and choose, anxious and scrambling.

The years are punctuated by more dramatic losses, the deaths of those for whom we truly care. Most of us know well what we'll wear to the next funeral.

Deep grief is a special case: a season in hell. We come to it when we lose someone we have set as our foundation, someone with whom and around whom we have built our lives and our identity. Along with the beloved teacher, child, parent, or partner, we lose our very selves.

Valerie Stephens was diagnosed with breast cancer in 2004 and with metastatic disease in 2012. She died in 2013. We had been married twenty-eight years; we had two young adult children.

Soon after she died, a friend wrote, "You set forth on a voyage into another realm; be sure to bring us back a record." Indeed I had entered a hidden world, a world coiled up tight inside the ordinary life-space of supermarkets and highways—a world where I stumbled, for a while, blind and raw. Could I somehow map it?

My friend offered a mission, the prospect of doing something useful. As a Buddhist practitioner, I could examine my grief as an object, a curious specimen under the mindfulness microscope. And in that way I could separate myself from it. But for the first few months, my concentration was such that I could scarcely write a sentence.

And we already have some impressive records of harrowing grief. It is commonplace, all around us, every day; we each have our turn in horror. Only a few will wonder what I mean—and they will come to know. We are all posttraumatic, pretraumatic, or—most often—both.

From within our grief-world our private pain feels like a singularity, as though with no bones we collapse, cut off from the willfully unwitting inhabitants of the utterly oblivious world. In my case, I felt as though I were undergoing something extremely strange, like a secret LSD experiment. I was alienated from everyone who seemed not to have been, or could not acknowledge being, in this world of utter loss.

This book is about that isolating sense of specialness. It is about awakening from the delusion that our pain is a private prison.

Another friend emailed me that his long engagement

with the Buddhist tradition was of no avail when his father died. This disappointed him. Unlike many others, he urged upon me no prayers, meditations, or mantra recitations. He wanted only to know: Was the Dharma helping me? What helped, how much, in what ways?

This is always the right question: What helps? That was the seed. I hope there will be some benefit from its fruit.

This Book

This book is an odd duck. I reflect on Buddhist practices and Buddhist ideas that were—and sometimes were not—of aid to me in the throes of loss. I make some suggestions about how we might help one another.

But it is unlike anything I have published before. My usual voice as a scholar and teacher presents the Dharma—particularly Tsongkhapa's Tibetan reading of Madhyamaka—in a relatively accessible manner. Some have taken that voice to represent fully my own perspective; it does not. I have received with deepest gratitude teachings from many traditional teachers. Yet readers will find that my sense of karma is not that of a traditional Tibetan Buddhist. My reflections engage with many Buddhist lineages but do not transmit the views of anyone else. Dharma is universal, flourishing in ways that are helpful in each time and place.

Here I write as a human passed well beyond the middle of the road of life. This is a personal account, an artifact of a painful time. My hope is that when you are in anguish, you will know that you are not alone. And when you meet those in anguish, you will help them to know that they are not alone.

The Structure of This Book

Loss is a universal experience, but each loss is particular. In many ways, my story arises from my relationship with Valerie Stephens. For this reason, I include a eulogy at the end of this book. At the end there are also acknowledgments and, in lieu of footnotes, brief narratives identifying my sources chapter by chapter.

Pain

The pervasiveness of grief-pain is a national secret. We never learned this fact of life in high school health class. We catch mention of others' losses, but our psychosocial immune system spares us the graphic details. The secret is not kept by the government but by all of us from one another. We conspire in diversionary conversation about shopping, weather, sports—and most especially the misdeeds of other people.

It is considered socially proper to hide the full measure of our pain, sometimes even from ourselves. "Really, now," inner voices declaim, "can't we talk about something more pleasant over dinner? Can't we have something more uplifting in our Dharma talk?" When we fail to don the mask, we invite being regarded as gloomy and self-involved.

There are so many types of loss, and we feel them in so many different ways. Sometimes grief is a state of utter shock. It can be like a blow to the head, or like an explosion, or like drowning.

Sick

In October 2012 Valerie came home from work, dropped her bag at the door, and wept. "I don't think I can do this any more. There is something really wrong with me."

She asked me to take her to the emergency room the next day . . . so I took her right then. The doctor on duty examined her and ordered a scan. After two hours he came back, the bad news in his expression. She had cancer throughout her bones, liver, and peritoneum. Metastatic breast cancer—quite advanced. Her condition was bad, with no prospect of cure. Without treatment she would live only weeks. With treatment, she would be more comfortable and, perhaps, live a bit longer.

Valerie was distraught. At a loss, the doctor turned on his heel and left us alone. After a while, I went out and asked that someone give us some guidance. They arranged an appointment at an oncology clinic.

Home after midnight, numb . . . unconscious for two hours. At 3:30 A.M. we awoke together, minds racing. Scribbling frantic lists of what we needed to do to close her clinical practice, tell her clients, and tell our family and her family and my family (in what order?), tell my employer and our friends. Long lists. We planned our withdrawal from almost everything in every part of our lives. First: I had to tell the kids, Gabe and Becca.

Most of the weekend we cried together. But Valerie had to spend hours each day alone on the phone, contacting each of her thirty clients privately, breaking the news. She closed immediately and permanently her clinical practice as a psychologist. Many clients were in shock and distressed for Valerie. Others were terrified for themselves: Where would they turn, given their desperate need for ongoing therapy? She called her colleagues and made referrals.

In the last year of her life Valerie dedicated herself to me, Gabe, and Becca. We managed her medications and got her to appointments; she focused her healing powers on us, preparing each of us for what lay ahead and binding us more closely together as a family. Money she had saved for retirement went for a series of family trips that functioned as retreats: just the four of us, each panicked in our own way, struggling to support one another.

Over that last year, Valerie was the most grounded person in any room, compassionate and forbearing. When friends visited, she would ask them about *their* lives and sometimes delicately offer a bit of tactful advice. Often the conversation turned so that she was helping them prepare for her death—and by extension, helping them to prepare for their own unforeseen deaths.

And she was good-humored. Her immune system was depleted by chemo and it seemed an impressive instance of mind over body that none of us got any colds or infections that would stop us from being near her. Overhearing us comment on this, Valerie chimed in: "And I haven't been sick at all either . . . except for the terminally ill part!"

Dying

In autumn 2013, Valerie switched to a third type of chemo-
therapy because the cancer had stopped responding to the
first two. Within a few weeks, she was walking a bit dif-
ferently, shuffling a bit. A side effect? Months before, a
hospice doctor and friend in the Dharma had warned me
that patients and families often mistake deadly symptoms
for chemo side effects.

Two days later, she had an intense headache. I took
her to the emergency room where an ER doctor quickly
pronounced that she had advanced brain cancer. How
could he presume to know something so terrible?

But he did. After a scan and a long wait, her oncologist
arrived to explain. Valerie had had asymptomatic brain
metastases all along. The earlier chemotherapies—chosen
simply for their milder side effects—just happened to be
ones that could pass the blood-brain barrier. They had
kept the brain metastases in check, but this new chemo
did not. She had extensive malignant meningioma, cancer
of the membrane surrounding the brain.

I have had flashbacks of this scene, especially around
3:30 A.M.:

> Oncologist: There is nothing we can do.
> Valerie: Nothing?
> Oncologist: It is advanced and widespread.
> Valerie: How long?
> Oncologist: Two or maybe three weeks.

While arranging hospice, the hospital admitted Valerie. The first night, she abruptly—and permanently—lost the ability to keep down anything taken orally. Now that she really was dying, her presence in the hospital created an administrative catch-22. Policy requires that patients not be released until they can take medication orally . . . but this was never going to happen. They kept giving her medicine and food by mouth. She kept vomiting. Dying people can be inconvenient.

Valerie kept her wits and her heart. She told me how sorry she felt for the nurses working our floor. They cared for us and wanted to help but were under orders from doctors who were complying with policies designed by lawyers and insurance companies, all with the aim of minimizing legal liability. Saving money. We agreed to stay a second night, but I told the resident that if he did not discharge her in the morning we would leave against medical advice. Those are magic words.

On the ride home Valerie's conversation became—for the first time—disorganized. She referred to Gabe by the name of her late brother. I soaked in with full attention these last moments with her as a whole person. We talked about the ways we had helped each other. I told her that she had done much more for me than I had for her. She mustered the energy to disagree. Pulling into the driveway, for some reason, I said: "It's you and me." And, in a dreamlike way, she answered: "Yep." And that was it.

She collapsed into bed. Over the next two days she had a few, flickering moments of lucidity, saying goodbye to her children. After another round of midnight patient advocacy, hospice set up intravenous steroids and pain medicine at home. Gabe, Becca, and I took shifts, turning her to avoid bedsores and pushing meds through the line. My siblings flew in, one by one, each doing a few days of stalwart support.

Early in the morning of November 19, Valerie stopped breathing. The hospice staff came out to help me clean and dress her, or to dress her body, or to dress *the* body. They helped me dress the body that had vividly seemed to be Valerie. Now it was her and yet not her. It was dead Valerie. Gabe and Becca and I stayed very close, touching her as she got cold. Then we invited a few friends over, one at a time, to say goodbye.

Grief

In the early months after Valerie died, my body felt as though I had a bad flu. I had whole-body aches and spells of violent shaking. This intense shivering was weird and baffling, until I found in grief literature that this is among the normal things that can happen. There was a constant, hollow sensation in my gut, something that felt desperate to be eased in a sigh. Yet sighing did not ease it at all.

My head felt as though I had a concussion. At first, I could concentrate just well enough to read two or three sentences at a time. I dashed about, as though manic, constantly forgetting what I was trying to do. There are an astonishing number of things to be done when a partner dies; it is hard to imagine until you have been through it. These "death duties" are actual responsibilities, sometimes important. But the frantic busyness also affords the bereaved a tempting defense against pain.

Sometimes waves of pain hit. Grief often flows—not in neat stages, but in the manner of surf and tides. I wrote:

> After a lull, waves
> Rush up and whiten the shore—
> Where has my friend gone?

I pulled off my wedding ring after the memorial service in late January. Someone asked about it and I said, "I can't be married to a ghost." But I was haunted. If a grief pang hit while I was alone, I would just scream a bit. Not that it helped much, but it felt necessary to call out to her or for her presence/absence. In early March I was feeling better, but still wrote:

> Ring finger bone ache:
> Not thinking dead or alive,
> Just calling for you.

In these early months I most often felt numb; I was disinterested in most of the activities that we take to constitute "living." My ordinary sense (or ordinary illusion) of my self as a real person did not operate.

Lit stark by death, our pastimes are futile. How can we fret about the weather or sports or the state of the stock market? Kobayshi Issa points out:

Even the beggar has a favorite wrestler.

But do the raw bereaved, with their death-denial reflexes impaired, actually care who wins at sumo or soccer? How was everyone else managing to conspire in this monumental pretense?

I sought hints that deep down they knew: the weary, anxious space between one game and the next, the uneasy moment when a joke falls flat. When the Buddha silently held up a flower, one person smiled—but what did everyone else feel? Not just puzzlement, but perhaps a kind of premonitory ache.

Many of us are addicted to the chase for evanescent pleasure. Others seek refuge via absorption in some fascinating obsession. Rather than face death and consider how best to make our short lives meaningful, the best we can manage is distraction. We fritter away precious hours, like kids playing hooky along the tracks, heads down and a dark worry shut up in our guts.

I slept three hours or less each night. I saw (and sometimes still see) everyone around me as corpses-to-be. We would rather not consider it, but humans are of two types: the dead and the soon-to-be-dead. I saw the contours of skullbones instead of, as is socially appropriate, looking only at the surfaces of faces. I had never much before engaged the charnel ground meditations, but now they were involuntary.

> If a monk, in whatever way, sees a body thrown in the charnel ground and reduced to bones gone rotten and become dust, he thinks of his own body thus: "This body of mine, too, is of the same nature as that body."

When Valerie entered hospice, colleagues covered my classes at the university. But after she died I had to grade the final exams. This was a slow torment because I had almost no mental focus. In January I was nominally back at work full time. Sometimes I went through the proper motions. Often, I forgot what I was supposed to be doing.

One exception to my new incompetence: in the classroom, a Guy-as-teacher persona popped up and engaged the students with apparent enthusiasm. The effect of some decades of habit, this persona ran automatically. It was strange to watch these performances so utterly different from my inner catatonia. It dawned on me that the students had no idea that I was a staggering zombie. This teaching persona expounded the Dharma in above-average form. Watching from within, I had a wry thought: "Not bad; whoever this fellow is, he seems to know a little something about impermanence."

My concentration slowly improved so that I could read a paragraph or a page at a time. The shivering abated. I learned to manage the insomnia. For better or worse, an incoherent stream of mental events slowly coagulated into a sense of being *a person*.

As with an adolescent identity crisis, I was uncertain who this person was. But one thing was immediately clear: he had inherited sole parental responsibility for two young adults who had just lost their mother. It hurt to know they had been worrying about their father.

My lawyer, whom I had chosen mainly on account of the fact that his wife had died, helped me understand that having a connection with and responsibility for children can help with grief.

When it is so evident that others need you, you are less likely to despair.

And, in truth, there are always those who need our help.

Intimacy

In *Zen Master Raven*, Robert Aitken writes:

> Woodpecker asked: "Do you think I could be a teacher?" Raven looked her over. "What's the dark side?" he asked. Woodpecker hesitated. "I'm not sure there is one," she said. Raven turned away, saying, "Then how can you be a teacher?"

Marriage may be a gravely serious yogic discipline. The limitation of this practice is that it creates a special class for whom one cares above all others. The Dalai Lama writes:

> Love toward your husband, wife, children, or a close friend is often mixed with attachment and when your attachment changes, your kindness may disappear.

Healthy attachment can rigidify and stratify such that there are a few for whom we care greatly, friends and kin for whom we care somewhat, strangers and neutral persons whom we ignore—and our actual enemies. When we see distress, our caring fades along this spectrum and warps into viciousness toward enemies. We may become so inflamed as to feel that even torture is a noble activity.

On the other hand, it is only from a basis of secure care that we become able to reach out to others. The love I give the world has roots in times when I learned that I am loveable. Family is one way to create the growth-medium for love within ourselves—and for the next generation. Valerie and I worked with and for one another, and our kids, to create a community of care.

Valerie was my heart companion. There was a resonance between us that rang deeper and clearer over the years. Of course, she had been wounded. Within a few weeks of meeting her, I was amazed to see how well she knew the raw spots in her own personality. She neither advertised them nor denied them. She knew their roots but made no excuses. She often reproached herself, but without a trace of self-condemnation. This basic sanity gave me confidence in her as a partner.

Rushing out to help others, we wannabe-bodhisattvas often trip on what we refuse to see in ourselves. How do our unresolved personal issues distort our interactions with those whom we seek to help? What do I seem to see in them that is really not about them at all, but rather a lost chapter—a hidden chapter—of my own story?

Teachers are not self-existent; they cannot be teachers on their own. There are teachers only in dependence on those ready to learn. And a real teacher must know her or his dark side. Don't trust a therapist who has not been in therapy or a healer who claims never to have been wounded. All of our good spiritual teachers have relied on good spiritual teachers.

This is why I like it when teachers are open about their vulnerabilities. To trust, I need a human model, an imperfect model, someone whose character is an unfinished masterwork. For instance, in *Zen Master Raven*, Robert Aitken writes:

> One morning Porcupine came to Raven privately and asked, "What is Raven Roshi?" Raven said, "I have this urge to prey upon newborn lambs."

In response to a wave of Zen sex scandals, Aitken acknowledged that he had sometimes had moments of lust toward young, female students. He explained that to notice this is itself Dharma practice. Using that energy in a constructive, nonharmful way is deeper practice. And, when it becomes helpful, even teaching about such imperfection can be a great practice of kindness.

Buddhist tradition records that when Devadatta tried to kill the Buddha by pushing a boulder onto him, a rock fragment cut the Buddha's toe. The bleeding was difficult to stop and the Buddha retired into a cave—where he had been meditating—to lie down and to wait for assistance.

Some of us prefer a transcendent and invulnerable Buddha, a Buddha who doesn't bleed. This view dominates Tibetan Buddhism. But notice: even in the account of the Buddha as a divine being, the manifestation of a vulnerable human teacher is a skillful means of caring for others.

The Dalai Lama, asked how he felt when hearing of atrocities in Tibet, said:

> Sometimes I get a little angry . . . but then it
> very quickly turns into compassion.

The initial acknowledgment of anger links my mind to the teacher. Rage and anguish and lust are deep-rooted; the teacher models how to work with them.

Family Practice

In raising children, my naive instinct was to trust myself, which meant to trust in a lazy, complacent way the models I had internalized as a child. Valerie, on the other hand, was determined not to replicate the past mindlessly. Her approach was grounded in the study of best practices, what research in child development indicated. When dying, well aware of my tendency to discursive distraction, she commended them to me, that I should keep them always in my heart.

For Valerie, separating from Gabe and Becca was an excruciating part her illness; it tormented her that she would not see them through the next stages of their lives.

We all felt and feel this keenly. Recently, Becca needed a medical test under anesthesia, and—wondering who would drive her home—the nurse asked, "Who is with you today, dear? Your mother?" Well, yes, but not in the way you mean. Her memory and the hard shape of her absence are always right here.

Writing to a layman, Dogen advises:

> When you find your place where you are, this is where practice occurs . . . for the place, the way, is neither large nor small, neither yours nor others.

Valerie and I found a place, a Dharma position, in one another and in raising kids together. This type of practice demands attention and focus—and growth in the capacity for selfless care.

She was not a Buddhist; I am. But we are all apprenticed to the same master—reality. We all suffer needlessly because we don't see things as they are. Half-blind, we rattle through a bruising world. Our common Dharma is the school of hard knocks, where we gradually, painfully, open our eyes.

Practice goes against the surge of our impulses to turn away. Getting up early to get kids fed, dressed, and off to school, chanting, wiping noses, meditating, going to committee meetings . . . Nothing good happens fast. Training is repetition. Opening the heart is hard work. We need lots of reps solving problems, breaking down defenses, softening up the tough hide of ego.

To love others we must love ourselves, wish well for ourselves, and then gradually learn to see others as similar cases of beings who, just like ourselves, want happiness and don't want suffering. But the first step, loving ourselves, can be notoriously hard. We become well able to love ourselves because another living being has fostered within us a capacity for loving connection.

Knowing that you are held in another's loving heart: this is what gives you the chance to become a whole person. We have the opportunity to become agents who intentionally observe, reflect upon, and modify our own thoughts and feelings.

The love of a well-attuned mother serves as the implicit model for the bodhisattva's skillful love for all living beings. Kensur Lekden advises:

> One should reflect on the delightful ways a mother holds a baby to her flesh, giving her milk . . . Except for having the shape of a human being, the child is like a helpless bug. She teaches it each word one by one, how to eat, sleep, put on clothes, urinate, and defecate. If one's mother had not taught these, one would still be like a bug.

Hundreds of other Tibetan texts give the same message. Tsongkhapa, for example, says:

> When you were a helpless, newborn infant, she held you to the warmth of her flesh . . . She

suckled you at her breast, used her mouth to give you soft food and remove mucus from your nose, and used her hand to wipe away your excrement . . . When you were hungry and thirsty, she gave you food and drink . . .

And:

When you suffered from illness, pain, or threat of death, your mother chose from the depths of heart that she would rather be sick than you be sick, rather be in pain than you be in pain, rather die than you die. Putting these feelings into action, she did what was needed . . .

Just as mothers (and others) have loved and cared for us, so we should care for them by helping others to flourish and find peace. We truly care for others by working from a wide and secure base—the deep conviction that *we are loveable*. We are worthy of love. Here is a story of how it happened in one family:

When my daughter was just shy of eighteen months, I was the parent who woke in the night to her frantic cries of Mommy, Mommy. When she saw me opening the door to her room, she was furious: "Bad Daddy, I hate you! Get Mommy." Hardly the reception I had hoped for at three in the morning. Tense, trying to be heard over her screams, I told her with an edge in my voice that Mommy was sleeping and that I was not going to wake her. But then I found myself softening as I suddenly felt, saw, tuned in to the logic of her behavior: if she were loud enough, she would get her mother. I found myself getting calmer and immediately, without thinking about it, I mirrored her rage with an exaggerated "mean face" accompanied by a tiny growl to mark my display as "pretend."

As the father understands his daughter's feelings, his own feelings change. This frees him to mirror her feelings back, to show her by his display that he knows what she is feeling. She can see herself in the mirror of his vocal and facial responses.

I then said, "awwnhh," voicing real sympathy with the need and disappointment beneath her anger. Listening, I then heard her repeating a new phrase beneath her tears: "Daddy, make me feel better." We shared a hug, we shared a song—and she went back to sleep for the night.

The child can see that her father feels with and for her, that he understands and wants to help. And in that moment, her distress is no longer overwhelming. It is not isolating. Without some version of such care, we are swamped by waves of emotional reactions. Or else we manage life only by completely cutting off all awareness of emotion.

But when we know well that we are loveworthy, then we feel safe even with painful emotions. We can know them *as* emotions, as transient mental states we can work with rather than mistaking them for reality itself. We are informed by and about our sadness and anger rather than compelled into action by them.

Some of us get what we need from our parents. Others get it later from teachers, spiritual mentors, friends, or partners who see and reflect our precious hearts. Such is the medium in which we grow.

Attainment

The measure of our growth is effective kindness to others and to ourselves. Spiritual attainment is not some special meditative experience. People can bliss out in a great many ways. To what end? Practice is morally helpful or else false. If we are not becoming at least a bit more kindhearted, then we are wasting these precious lives.

Mary Oliver counsels herself:

> Am I no longer young and still half perfect?
> Let me keep my mind on what matters . . .

It is sad to think about getting older and older and attaining only to snarling, bitter jealousy of those younger or richer or healthier. Or . . . perhaps we will envy those who are more kindhearted!

Each breath we draw is one less left. *What are we doing?*

George Saunders told a graduating class at Syracuse that his greatest regret is that he failed to protect a girl who was being bullied in his grade school. Let's resolve, each morning, not to miss our chances this particular day. And if we do miss a chance, let us regret that and resolve to be kindhearted and skillful the next day, and the next day after that.

Valerie and I made kindness and honesty the core of our family practice. Perhaps this sounds too simple to be the Dharma, but it is the Dharma. Ordinary acts of loving consideration, as between parent and child, are the roots of the mature dedication of Great Helpers of living beings. Pema Chödrön agrees:

> As long as we don't want to be honest and kind with ourselves, we will always be infants . . . Gradually, without any agenda except to be honest and kind, we assume responsibility for being here in this unpredictable world, in this unique moment, in this precious human body.

In order to be of help, we have to be honest to the marrow about what is really here, who we really are: We are vulnerable. We are mortal. We are selfish. We are in pain. This is hard to look at.

But hard-won honesty does not justify being grim, negligent, or cruel in order to reflect, in a genuine way, our actual, immature mental state. This is a troubling misstep. Someone asked Jeffrey Hopkins why he was constantly talking about training in compassion. "Just be yourself!" she suggested. Jeffrey answered:

> Maybe that would work for you, but without some such effort I would mainly care for myself, even at the expense of others.

Robert Aitken, himself a father, found this insight in a deep dream:

> Black Bear came to a meeting late and said, "I'm feeling frazzled after dealing with the cubs. What if I don't feel compassionate?" Raven said, "Fake it." "That doesn't seem honest," said Black Bear. "It doesn't begin with honesty," said Raven.

We honestly don't want to go to work sleep-deprived after caring for a colicky baby or a young child with night terrors. It doesn't start with honesty if so-called honesty is a pretext for denying others care that they critically need.

Yet to take care of others, we must remember to care for ourselves. We are among those worthy of compassion. Not mistaking the state of our hearts, we train in tenderness toward both others and ourselves.

And good intentions are not enough; we must be fully present and skillfully responsive. Our caring draws us ever into new terrain. We keep learning things we never thought would matter, things we need to give care in certain moments:

> The man is a father now. He knows the names
> of all the neighborhood dogs.

Yet we so often wound those who are closest, so conveniently at hand as targets! They are most vulnerable to us because we know their weak points. And they threaten us because they can see—and make us face—our faults.

Like everyone else, Valerie had her issues. And we were different in many ways. Often these differences were complementary, but at other times they made our marriage tough training. Our kinship of heart was always there, so we helped each other grow by working with even our sharpest differences.

Valerie knew how much she was loved, and so allowed herself to be seen in her perfect imperfection. We opened to one another, so that now I feel her presence even in my bones. Yet that presence is a shadow, the unique shape of her unending absence.

The Great Matter

> Priest Jianyuan of Tan once accompanied his teacher, Daowu, on a condolence call to a family funeral. When they arrived, he tapped the coffin and said, "Is this life, or is this death?"
> Daowu said, "I won't say life, I won't say death."
> Jianyuan said, "Why won't you say?"
> Daowu said, "I won't say, I won't say."

If you say things never change, don't you violate the truth of experience? Valerie breathing, Valerie *never breathing again*: no change?

But when you try to explain exactly *what* changes, things get murky. We want to dodge the question. In the dialogue above, Daowu did not clam up or dodge. He poured out his guts on the matter of life in the face of death. This isn't easy to see.

As a young man, before I met Valerie, I was in a relationship with Joan for many years. She began to have recurrent forebodings and a persistent sense of déjà vu. Then: she got lost driving across town. It was frightening, but no doctor could say what was going on. Eventually a cardiologist found a tumor in the right temporal lobe of her brain. Along with her family, I cared for her—and one night I watched her die.

I was scarcely able to function. My graduate studies in Buddhism stalled and I botched my first teaching job. Separating from Joan seemed to eviscerate me. Day after day, I sensed myself as hollow, like an abandoned shell.

Eighteen months later I dreamt of a tree that had been cut into very deeply but not cut down. The tree grew, year after year, and there was always a scar. It would always be marked. But the scar's shape and size in relation to the growing tree kept changing. A time came when it was not the main thing you noticed when you looked at the tree. And later, the scar was so integral to the tree that you could not recognize it as having been a wound. This was so clear: I could never stop being the person who loved and lost Joan. Now I would see what that person could become next.

Often this sort of issue complicates grief. After a talk, a troubled woman came to me with her story. Her husband died four years ago. She goes out dancing, but when she touches a man she thinks of her husband. She freezes up —and relapses into grief. I also met a young woman whose mother died when she was an adolescent. Her emotional development stalled because she did not want to grow past the age when she and her mom were together.

Like the tree in my dream, we are never in danger of becoming unmarked by our past. We can't shake it as easily as we might fear or hope. What has happened will always have happened; it cannot unhappen. Death cannot touch the actuality of the past. Derek Parfit writes:

> When someone I loved died I found it helpful to remind myself that this person was not less real because she wasn't real now, just as people in New Zealand aren't less real because they aren't real here.

This is sound philosophy. Consider that Martin Luther King Jr.—having lived and affected the world—will always *have been*, and his having been is a crucial constituent of the world now, and now, the world as it appears in each new moment. He is not and can never become unreal and imaginary in the manner of unicorns or square circles.

On a different scale, the same is true of Valerie and all the loved ones we have lost. Their having-been is ineradicable—and it *matters*. Utter loss is impossible; we don't need to exacerbate the pain by seizing up in panic. We will always be in relationship with them. And as our loved ones have loved us, they have wished well for us. This remains a fact.

We honor them by being kind to ourselves.

Feeling Bad about Feeling Bad

Last year, I met a young man who was distraught—and in further distress about being distraught. He had cheated and destroyed his marriage . . . and felt especially terrible because, he said, he was stuck "wallowing" in grief. "How long ago did this happen?" I wondered. "Six weeks," he said, in a tone suggesting this had been an eon. But that is not wallowing; that is mourning. Pain is natural after a great loss.

And when we have hurt others, or missed a chance to be kind, the pain of regret is healthy. I have been a primary caretaker for three dying people: Joan, my father, and Valerie. In each case, as an imperfect being, the best that I could do for them as they were dying was imperfect. I made mistakes; I sometimes missed the mark. Notice regret and resolve to do better. If no restitution is possible, give others now the sort of care you wish you had already given.

We need a middle way: not denying the actuality of our pain, while not identifying with it as our core self. If we think, "*I* am the one who remembers and dwells in pain," "*I* am the one who lost his wife," then it recycles again and again. Samsara. It is like someone constantly picking off a scab. When we have deep pain that seems not to touch others, we get sucked into this sense that pain is our deepest identity. Intense anguish feels as though it were our private, secret, inner selfhood.

On the other hand, don't avoid what is happening. Don't try to bury your pain. Indeed, one friend advocated this to me as his approach and the approach of everyone in his family: "Keep your head down." Plow ahead. Bull your way into the future, without being waylaid by sentiment. Oddly, while this may seem like the opposite of identifying with your pain, it is not. Hiding your head does not make it go away. Repressed pain returns, reborn again and again in new forms.

Sitting with Valerie's cooling body: looking at the pain is like staring at the sun. But pushing it away won't help. We have to do what we can, feeling out what more might be possible. Keep your head up, your eyes open to see what is even a bit helpful—and then what might be another bit more helpful. As we get more able to watch pain with a bare mind, not identifying with it, we may see it slowly ebb. It is not a constant—quite the opposite. "How I feel" is not only difficult to express, it is also a fast-moving target. It is not disloyal to have moments when you don't feel bad. Should I happen to laugh now and then, it is definitely not a sin!

There will be a new, less painful mental state—and then that also will slip away. To be human is to set sail for the next shipwreck. Soko Morinaga writes:

> When a preschooler loses a tooth, a still more wonderful tooth comes to take its place, but when a grown-up loses one, it stays lost! Death comes to take away the friends you have so deeply cherished. The children, for whom you sacrificed your own food and clothing, leave the

> parental nest. Then retirement rolls around, and the job over which you have taken such pains must be relinquished. You begin to forget what you thought you had learned. You lose the muscles you laboriously built up, and they never really return. No matter how a person looks at it, one comes to feel acutely that human life is not a matter of gaining, but of losing.

But wait. Aren't Buddhists supposed to have transcended grief? What were we expecting? Was the Buddha not clear enough? We just need to "let go."

When I was a young instructor at Mary Washington College, a student paper shocked me by arguing that Vietnamese Buddhists do not mourn their dead family members because they know that they are going on to future lives. Giving this writer skillful guidance was my first big teaching challenge.

Most of us would not think this way, but we may fall into subtler missteps. Having met some Dharma and engaged it, many come to feel that they have taken death and impermanence into account.

We might have. But probably not. Like everyone else, Buddhists seldom die as they expect. We die in some other way, too soon or too late, in ways we never imagined. We die in fear, and sadness, and in disappointment. Death is what happens when we are making other plans. And if our lives are committed to service, we will die while we still have critical work to do.

When Dainin Katagiri Roshi was dying of cancer, he told his frightened students, "I see you are watching me closely; you want to see how a Zen master dies. I'll show you." He kicked violently and screamed, "I don't want to die!" Then he looked at them: "I don't know how I will die . . . Remember, there is no right way." None of us know how we will face death.

Let's not fool ourselves. Meditation on death and impermanence does not magically make us invulnerable or transhuman. Losing those we love hurts. When his daughter died of smallpox, Kobayashi Issa wrote:

> The world of dew
> Is indeed a world of dew.
> And yet, and yet . . .

Issa comments on his poem:

> I knew that it was no use to cry, that water once flown past the bridge does not return and scattered blossoms are gone beyond recall. Yet try as I would, I could not, simply could not cut the binding cord of human love.

The Buddha teaches that all that arises is ephemeral, vanishing like a drop of dew in the morning sun. And this is true. Issa cannot evade the full force of this fact; as a Buddhist, he has long known this well—or thought he had. Now this little girl's death hurts him bone-deep, cuts him to the core. To be utterly heart-wrecked and, at the same time, strangely grateful for some lost grace—this is what it will always mean to be a human who loves another mortal.

So we may have unrealistic expectations about how well our practice has prepared us to die or to lose someone whom we love more than our own lives. We may feel worse than we had expected to feel. You are practicing, your spouse dies—and suddenly it seems as though someone clubbed you in the head. Your grief may be complicated by useless disappointment in yourself—or in the Dharma itself.

One woman came to me in a difficult grief after losing a parent. She made a commitment to intensive religious practice with the belief that she had taken the prospect of losing her parent into account. When grief hit her hard, she was doubly tormented. Because she felt so bad about her parent's death, she felt like a failure as a Buddhist.

Soko Morinaga tells a similar story. His friend Miss Okamoto was a dedicated Zen practitioner for decades, but as death approached she was terrified—and also profoundly ashamed of her terror.

I did not find my wife's death at all surprising. I had a vague idea that she would outlive me, but I also knew that she expected to die first. I wasn't startled that she died. And yet: I was shocked; it was a physical shock.

Shock does not have to involve surprise. It took me months to understand. It is like someone informing you that he is going to punch you in the head—and then punching you in the head. You're not surprised, but you do have a concussion.

Shock and pain are not a personal failure. It is cruel to judge ourselves so harshly; it is unhelpful to blame ourselves for being human.

Knowing the first noble truth does not exempt us from it.

Who Dies?

In the Buddhist tradition, we say that in the flow of change there is never any fixed thing we can point out that corresponds to the things named by our language. It's useful to think of things and people as though they had fixed identities, but they don't. They are like fast-rushing streams. And a table is just what we call a certain collection of table parts—none of which is itself a table. Every thing and person is what it is only in relation to a perspective, a point of view. Nothing exists as this or that from its own side. So everyone and everything is *empty* of existing in the way we usually see them.

For these reasons, Buddhists say that in an ultimate sense, there is no dying and no one who dies. Nagarjuna's *Treatise on the Middle Way* opens with this homage:

> I prostrate to the Perfect Buddha,
> The best of teachers, who taught that
> Whatever is dependently arisen is
> Unceasing, unborn,

> Unannihilated, not permanent,
> Not coming, not going,
> Without distinction, without identity
> And free from conceptual construction.

Anything that is contingent, including our human lives, has a fundamental nature of neither coming nor going, not beginning, not ending. As Gary Snyder puts it, needless misery arises from clinging to the notion that "things can be gained and lost whereas in truth all is contained vast and free in the Blue Sky and Green Earth of One Mind."

The grave difficulty is how this "nothing is lost" perspective pertains to the brutal fact that Valerie has lost her life. She was here and now is not. I am still here, now without her. She definitely did not want to die; her friends and family and doctors all wished that she would not die. Yet the Chan tradition instructs:

> The great way is without difficulty.
> Just don't pick and choose.
> Neither love nor hate
> And you will clearly understand.

Don't pick and choose? Between Valerie being alive and Valerie being *dead?*

I have to remind myself that these wisdom teachings arise from, are transmitted through, and revered by *human beings.* They don't radiate from a Divine Creator or an alien intelligence; they are not output from a computer.

Yet they cut ragged against the grain of common sense and human feeling. It is starkly clear that the Dharma does not "go with the flow." It does not offend us with platitudes or insult us with cheap consolation. Pema Chödrön says:

> We are completely changing our way of per-
> ceiving reality, like changing our DNA. We are
> undoing a pattern that is not just our pattern. It
> is the human pattern that we project onto the
> world.

Or as Don Lopez puts it:

> The Buddha . . . presented a radical challenge
> to the way we see the world . . . What he taught
> is not different, it is not an alternative, it is the
> opposite. That the path that we think will lead
> us to happiness leads instead to sorrow. That
> what we believe is true is instead false. That
> what we imagine to be real is unreal.

So it is that when someone asked me in the early months whether my familiarity with Buddhist teachings on empti-ness had consoled me in my grief, my reflexive answer was just no. All I could think was that Valerie, empty or not, was definitely around here before and now she is definitely not. And that hurts.

To deny this is to miss the Middle Way. Those who think emptiness cancels out this fact cannot have understood.

Valerie was here; now she is not. This is true and it hurts. It must not be denied.

But this is not the *only* thing that is true. Shunryu Suzuki teaches:

> After some years we will die. If we *just* think that it is the end of our life, this will be the wrong understanding. But, on the other hand, if we think that we do not die, this is also wrong. We die, and we do not die. This is the right understanding.

And Kosho Uchiyama sings:

> Though poor, never poor.
> Though sick, never sick.
> Though aging, never aging.
> Though dying, never dying.

The Buddha taught that the source of self-generated misery is an exaggerated sense of the self's reality. We futilely grasp at anything we mistake as a stable anchor against the void. We hurt in part because we clutch in desperation at what cannot be held at all, fearing to drown in the dark void. But in whatever way things cannot be truly held, they also cannot be truly lost.

In the Pali scriptures, the Buddha repeatedly addresses questions about whether awakened persons pass out of existence at the end of their final lifetimes. The Buddha takes no position and in one case remains silent. He explains that it would be misleading to say yes and misleading to say no, because the person cannot be pinned down as this or that. The particular *kind* of person we worry about, and fear for, can never be lost or harmed—because she has never existed at all.

And, of course, this is true not just of the awakened person. It is true of every person at the end of every lifetime. And it is *always* true of every person, as we stream instant by instant. In this way it is misleading even to say that things change. What are these *things*? Is there some stable, underlying person or thing that appears first in one way and then in another, and then in yet another? We think and talk in this way, but upon close inspection, the world is not like that at all.

Close inspection means paying attention to and reflecting on just this, our lived experience. It does not mean thinking about some *other* thing, truth or Buddha or God or emptiness. It means going deeply into whatever presents itself, wondering. It means not mistaking even our most helpful words—sound ideas and sacred stories—to be the measure of reality. During Valerie's illness and after her death, for some while, what I attended to and reflected upon was often disorientation, pain, and loss.

Siddhartha left home because he saw that he had no way to protect his family from sickness and death. But he found no magic in meditation or self-starvation; he found only a way to drop his fear and open his heart. What was that way? The meditation teacher Ajahn Chah was once

asked how he could be happy in this world of impermanence where we cannot protect those we love from harm,
illness, and death. He pointed to a beautiful glass, holding
water, glistening in the sun. One day an elbow or a strong
wind certainly will knock it over. *It is already broken.* We
can, therefore, use it in fearless freedom.

Death is safe—but only insofar as we can take the perspective that there is nothing to gain and nothing to lose.
There is nowhere else to go; there is just this.

Chuang Tzu counsels:

> You hide your boat in a ravine and your fishnet
> in the swamp and tell yourself that they will be
> safe. But in the middle of the night a strong man
> shoulders them and carries them off and in your
> stupidity you don't know why it happened. You
> think you do right to hide little things in big
> ones, and yet they get away from you. But if
> you were to hide the world in the world, so that
> nothing could get away, this would be the final
> reality of the constancy of things.

Of course, we unawakened folk rarely hold the whole
world safe within itself. We hear that nothing is ever really
gained or lost because from the outset nothing ever existed
in the way we imagined. And maybe we get a glimmer of
what that means. But mostly we build our lives, our selves,
around a particularly precious boat—a child, spouse,
friend, parent, or spiritual teacher—and we cradle it deep

in the ravine of our heart, in what we desperately wish were safety. But there comes irresistible circumstance— cancer or a tsunami or a disturbed person with a gun. The cradle breaks, the baby falls.

When our boat is gone, when our carapace is cracked and our hearts are wrecked, then we can see that *it is not just us*. And it is not just right now. Everyone is just like this. Everyone is mortally wounded. We are all defrauded by our own fairy tale. We are always already bereft of what we promise ourselves.

As Pema Chödrön says:

> This . . . is not just our personal misfortune, our fault, our blemish, our shame—it's part of the human condition. It's our kinship with all living things, the material we need to stand in another person's shoes.

So there is no one *else*, no one watching safely from the sidelines. Tolstoy's Ivan Ilyich finds it finally on his deathbed:

> All of [my life] was simply not the real thing . . . "But what *is* the real thing?" he asked himself and grew quiet, listening. Just then he felt some- one kissing his hand. He opened his eyes and looked at his son. He grieved for him.

When we see that we cannot be alone, that we are all in

the soup, then there comes to be another human way to love. It is a love that has parting sorrow in full view. Rainer Maria Rilke said that his greatest poetry was motivated by an aspiration to present "the transformations of love that are not possible where Death is simply excluded as the Other."

Nagarjuna puts it this way:

> From what is empty, comes what is empty—
> Including living beings, all they do,
> And everything they come up against.
> When we meditate on this,
> It is inevitable that we become attached
> To the welfare of others.

I know that these are not just words. They point right at an awful promise, a prophecy that Thoreau knew and pronounced:

> Not till we are lost, not till we have lost the world, do we begin to find ourselves, and realize where we are and the infinite extent of our relations.

Susan Bauer-Wu, a professor of nursing, is more concise: "Patients are not a special class of people. They're us."

For thirteen months I drove Valerie to a research hospital for treatment. Cancer patients surrounded us all day; we shared bagels. This woman is here with her young children and has just gotten a grave diagnosis. This older woman has been sick for ten years—and she is here in cancer land with no family support. Sun streams through a wide bay where the sick lie companionably side by side, getting infused with toxic dope. Everyone copes without any pretense that things are fine.

We're all broken and we all know it; no one is alone.

There is something strong in this unspoken intimacy.

Karma

In 2004, Valerie was diagnosed with breast cancer and, after some medical mishaps, had surgery. While she recovered, we often watched the Detroit Pistons play basketball on TV. We were a bit in shock and wondering how to make sense of what had hit us.

The Pistons won an NBA championship in part by trading for Rasheed Wallace, a fierce competitor raised in the most dangerous neighborhood in Philadelphia. When he believes the officials have erroneously charged him or a teammate with a foul, as his opponent stands at the free throw line, Wallace is apt to shout: "Ball don't lie!"

It struck me that Wallace views the free throw line as a sort of trial, as practiced in medieval Europe, where the accused is tested by being bound and dumped into water, or made to touch hot metal. Here it is the alleged victim of wrongdoing that is tested, being given an opportunity to prove that a crime was truly committed—this being demonstrated if and only if the punishment is consummated by a successful free throw.

Such beliefs—or at least the practice of proclaiming such beliefs—are a sort of folk tradition. It is folk theodicy, without the theism—except insofar as the ball and the line are basketball gods. Thus, in the sense in which Wallace seems to mean it, "ball don't lie" is a religious belief that the universe is fundamentally *fair*.

Was Valerie's cancer the moral consequence of some past action? Does the ball lie or not?

From the scholarly work of Clifford Geertz:

> The rain falls on the just
> And unjust fella,
> But mostly on the just
> As the unjust has the just's umbrella.

The ball never deceives, but neither do its bounces seem to adjudicate justly. I would tend to suppose that they do not adjudicate at all. If they did, then why would Valerie's cancer be any different? I cannot see it as the just outcome of her choices. Yet Wallace feels compelled to insist otherwise—and he is not alone. This is a recurring theme in world religions.

Religions often give adherents consolation that while the universe seems unjust—the ball seems to lie—really, in reality, ultimately, in God's eye, from the point of view of emptiness, there is some higher sense in which it does not or cannot lie. A naive appearance, as when our friend looks to be peacefully sleeping, is superseded by the reality of a hard worldly fact—she is dead. This hard worldly fact turns out to be a mere appearance in relation to a higher reality posited by religion—she looks dead, but her true self has immortal life. And this higher reality confirms—with a twist—the hopes implicit in the original naive appearance: she is at peace in the Lord. Or, he has gone to the Pure Land.

"Ball don't lie" is, then, another case like the Biblical teaching, "You will reap what you sow." And it is like some ways of teaching karma.

Nagarjuna's *Precious Garland* states:

> From nonvirtues come all sufferings
> And likewise all miserable realms.
> From virtues come all happy realms
> And the joys in all rebirths.

Tsongkhapa explains:

> All sufferings in the sense of painful feelings . . .
> arise from previously accumulated nonvirtuous
> karma.

So it is claimed that while people might lie about being victims, players might flop to deceive referees, referees themselves may be corrupt, biased, or nearsighted, in the end it does not matter because the universe (as locally manifest in the ball itself) is objective, impersonal, nondeceptive, and therefore, in some fundamental way, fair.

On this view, everyone always gets what they have coming.

On this view, Valerie got just what she had coming. In a sense, she died at her own hand because her past actions caused her cancer.

To me, this seems outrageous. There is no evidence for it, and it inflicts more pain on those in pain.

Strong Karma

Kobayashi Issa laments:

> It is a commonplace of life that the greatest pleasure issues ultimately in the greatest grief. Yet why—why is it that this child of mine, who has not tasted half of the pleasures that the world has to offer, who ought by rights to be as fresh and green as the vigorous young needles on the everlasting pine—why must she lie here on her deathbed, swollen with blisters?

It is agony for Issa to watch his young daughter die. It was agony to watch Valerie die.

The Dharma teaches that attachment to pleasure leads to grief, but what about these young innocents? What about Gabe and Becca? Does the Dharma allow us to understand every loss as fair in the particular sense of being naturally consequent to the sufferer's past choices?

It is clear that for a great many people such notions are both psychologically useful and morally helpful. Given the great difficulties that we have regulating our harmful actions, it may sometimes be skillful to consider our current miseries as outcomes of just such actions in the past.

What we do is very important. In great measure, what we choose to do makes us who we are now, and now, in a seamlessly streaming manner. As Pema Chödrön puts it:

> Every act counts. Every thought and emotion counts too. This is all the path we have.

This is how I understand the teaching of karma. This teaching is crucial to the future happiness of the world. I want to see it more fully accepted, universally accepted, more deeply understood.

But often a major obstacle to such faith is the notion that karma effectively guarantees that life is fair. This is an obstacle because many people find such notions utterly unsustainable in the face of lived experience. Issa—who knew all about karma—does not turn for consolation to the idea that his daughter had in the past done something terrible to cause her own illness. I have no reason to think Valerie caused her own cancer. And I find no comfort in imagining this to have been the case.

Nagarjuna warned that misunderstanding emptiness is dangerous, like mishandling a poisonous snake. We rarely encounter such warning labels on karma; we are admonished to have faith and drink deep. But the import of emptiness is precisely the dependent origination of the world, including karmic conditioning. So this Dharma medicine, like emptiness, needs careful handling.

Suppose we notify the victims of a tsunami that this is mainly a natural consequence of their own past wrongdoing. It is true that no God is judging them and they are not necessarily to blame in the usual sense. Yet proponents of what we could call "strong karma" will have to say: the tsunami that killed your family is the natural consequence of your past choices.

The Buddha taught that right speech is speech that is kind, meaningful, and true. It seems clear that making the strong karma claim in a case like this will very seldom be *kind* speech. And as for such speech being true, there is no evident factual basis for such a claim.

Yet people often say and believe such things. Sometimes they do it without deep analysis, because they want to be faithful to what their teacher has said, to be loyal to the Dharma as it has been transmitted to them. And they find comfort in believing that painful experiences arise very specifically from the sufferer's past wrongdoing. It eases their fear to imagine they are fully in control.

Our Choices Matter

The traditional notion is that when we choose to act we are, in a way, planting a seed. A good or bad experience in the future will arise from the germination of this seed. Good seeds—virtuous choices—lead to pleasurable effects; bad seeds to bad effects. But as the mindstream flows, there is no stable field as a lodging place for karmic seeds from the time of the action until they germinate as some new circumstance.

I find it much more helpful to picture waves and think about probability. A choice, an action, is like a wave in a field of energy, a ripple in a pond. It affects the next moment of our mind; it affects other people; it affects the world at large. Seeds seem static; karma is more like the dynamic reverberations of our past choices—some echoing longer and stronger than others.

Every event makes some kind of wave—some are massive and some are microripples. All of them condition, to widely varying degrees, other events. Our choices are one set of waves in a vast, churning sea. Waves will *usually* have the *greatest* effect right where they arose (within our mindstream) and in the moments right after they arose. As time passes or at greater distance, it is less likely that our choices will be the most powerful factor in play—although sometimes they may have great effects over vast regions. And all of our choices contribute to new environments that set the stage—serve as the field—for future waves.

Naturally, then, many situations come from the inter-action of our choices with the choices of others and with impersonal forces. Some effects are immediate results of our choices; often, we experience effects that are partly the results of our earlier choices. But sometimes we get rocked by the wake of another boat. It's a fact that we all get whacked by forces we did not set up. As with Issa's daughter. As with Valerie.

So our choices matter and cocreate the future, but they are not always the *main* causes of what happens to us. This is a realistic and helpful way to think about the world. What we do makes a difference, but it does not uniquely determine our future; no one has *that* much control! We cannot simply classify karma as individual or collective—it's all sloshing around, resonating and interfering.

Henry Melvill saw this when he wrote:

> Ye cannot live for yourselves; a thousand fibres connect you with your fellow-men, and along these fibres, as along sympathetic threads, run your actions as causes, and return to you as effects.

The world is astonishingly messy and rich, a teeming wilderness of possibilities tangled with trillions of con-necting threads. In the traditional metaphor of karma as a seed, what we reap is always just what we have sown. But on actual farms, farmers plant seeds as best they can without guarantees about the harvest. There are locusts and weeds. Sometimes good horticulture is ruined by a freak hailstorm.

So, what then? To be whole, we practice a clear-eyed sort of virtue. As Soko Morinaga says:

> Anytime and anywhere, the person who exerts himself or herself with dignity, without worrying about results and without giving in to disappointment, is a true practitioner, a true person of the Way. I believe that *just this* is the form of true human wellbeing.

My grandmother Alice worked day after day, year after year, to help poor women in El Salvador. But over time, due to factors *far* beyond her control, their plight grew much worse. In her work as a clinical psychologist, Valerie helped a great many clients. But some she was unable to help. A few got worse. It is hard to understand, and harder to accept, that in the world as it actually is, *we affect billions of things far into the future but we cannot fully control anything at all*. We promise to save all beings, but it will come to pass that our best efforts will not save even one person whom we love more than our own life. Issa could not save his child; I could not save Valerie. Yet the evidence of cultures around the world suggests most of us prefer self-condemnation to admitting what is terrifying and obvious: sometimes we are helpless.

It is simple, and sometimes encouraging, and so sometimes helpful, to say: "If you are in misery, look to your own past action." And of course the very worst danger is to give people the idea that their choices don't matter. There is nothing that matters more.

But often that confidence is harmed by the idea that all misery is due to the miserable person's past choices. This dogma discourages people from working to end unjust social systems. After all, who benefits from the claim, prior to consideration of any particular case, that a poor person must be poor due to his own past actions?

This idea also causes feelings of shame and guilt after painful events where the victim had no control. Do we really want to insist that all victims of atrocities suffer in consequence of their own past nonvirtue? David R. Loy reports hearing a Buddhist teacher comment on the Holocaust: "What terrible karma all those Jews must have had . . ." This is offensive. But it seems to me that if you hold the strong karma claim, you can fault that particular teacher only for being impolitic or unskillful. He was speaking what he takes as the Dharma.

I expect many of my dear friends will be saddened or outraged by what I write here. Many hold the strong karma claim at the center of their faith. But it is my conviction that teaching karma in that way is contrary to moral sense and sound reason. And so, over time, it will engender undue skepticism about the heart of this Dharma teaching: our choices matter and help shape the future.

Who Says that Life Is Fair?

The strong karma claim is found in Buddhist sutras as well as in the teachings of many great teachers. For example, the Mahayana sutra called *Samadhiraja*, or *King of Samadhis*, says:

> Once you have committed an action, you will
>   experience its effect;
> You will not experience the effects of actions
>   not committed.

So the Buddha seems to say that Valerie caused her own illness. But in the Pali scriptures, the Buddha says:

> When these ascetics and Brahmins have such a view and doctrine that "whatever a person experiences, be it pain, pleasure, or neutral feelings, all of that is caused by previous action," they go beyond what they know by themselves and what is accepted by the world. Therefore I say that this is wrong on the part of these ascetics and Brahmins.

These two reports are in contradiction. If we look to other scriptures to sort out which of these scriptures to rely upon, we will find that those too contain contradictions. As the Dalai Lama has pointed out, when scriptures contradict one another, our final recourse must be reasoned analysis.

And—unlike teachings on emptiness—teachings about karma are *provisional*. They serve a particular purpose, to help living beings in a particular way. They do not guarantee the justice of the universe.

In fact, there is no assurance that life—this one or any other—will be fair. Our actions shape our character and the course of our life, but they do so in constant interaction with innumerable other forces beyond our ken. A just balancing of the scales is a human ideal. When attained, it is a human attainment.

On the last ride home from the hospital Valerie whispered, "It's not fair," and I said, "No." Just an acknowledgment. The universe gave us no guarantee; it has no customer service number. There is no one to whom we can complain and, in the end, nothing to complain about.

Like Rasheed, we want to believe otherwise. And most of us, most of the time, would rather blame ourselves than admit that we cannot control when or how our loved ones die. So we really can't even complain about purveyors of the dream that life is fair. We were hoping to be persuaded; we pay them to say it. And meanwhile they themselves are frantically hoping that it is, in some way, true.

Knowing that we have this desperate wish, we should be wary of claims that our fantasy is fulfilled by the ultramysterious inner workings of karma. We can outgrow this hollow consolation. Our well-being, our dignity, is already fulfilled when we forget ourselves in acts of love.

Taking Care

If you don't tend to one another,
who then will tend to you?
THE BUDDHA

We all suffer needlessly because we don't see things as they are. I think this is the core idea of the Buddhist tradition.

The tradition invites us to consider the proposition that vast oceans of misery are unnecessary. And, more astonishingly, that there is a single cause at the root of needless misery—the delusion that things exist by way of their own natures. We are invited to consider that such delusion may be the tacit foundation for our daily quarrels and our bloody wars.

The Sanskrit word that most often represents this basic delusion is *avidya*, which is usually translated as "ignorance." To overcome ignorance, and become free from needless misery, we must in some way get to know things as they are.

These are good words, but they are just words and there are other helpful ways use words. When Valerie was dying, the book on our bed was Joan Halifax's *Being with Dying*. Halifax trains hospice workers using Buddhist insights, and her root framework is threefold: (1) not knowing, (2) bearing witness, and (3) compassionate action. So here the basic practice isn't *knowing*; rather, it is *not knowing*.

I'd been trained to think of the path in terms of progressive knowingness, deeper insight and understanding, so it was at first hard for me make sense of this. The words are contradictory, but the meaning is not. Of all the books about death and dying, *Being with Dying* was most helpful to me. At a time when I could scarcely think, it rang true. It sparked a small synaptic connection to Lao Tzu: "The farther you go, the less you know."

Not Knowing

When facing personal loss, or giving direct personal care, forget for a while what you think you know. Set aside every supposed solution, philosophical consolation, and religious device with which you have armed yourself. Forget Kübler-Ross's five stages. Drop all ideas about what is supposed to be happening or what you really ought to do. As Shunyru Suzuki says:

> In the beginner's mind there are many possibilities; in the expert's mind there are few.

Joan Halifax tells of a woman who, while dying, blissfully persists in saying, "I am not dying." Her friends are concerned, but Halifax doesn't try to fix it. We really *don't know* that it is delusion or denial—we don't know what this woman is experiencing. Maybe the "I" that is not dying is something that was never born and can never die. In the same way, Robert Aitken tells us:

> One evening Woodpecker asked, "What's the void?" Raven said, "Not the void." Woodpecker asked, "It's not really empty?" Raven said, "The truth is, I really don't know."

There is in presumed knowledge an arrogance that violates the moment. But the expert is unready to come naked to the moment. He arrives armed with information about what we feel and what we need to do and what will happen next. She officiously advises without invitation. Even a professional—lama, nurse, professor, or therapist—can disarm herself and approach empty-handed. On the other hand, the untrained may be seized by an expert mind. This is because the stance of *knowing* is a tempting defense against fear.

So it is understandable. But on the receiving end, unsolicited expertise often feels like a kind of violence. Valerie got an unsolicited discourse on the need to be grateful that she wasn't dying on the streets of India. She was firmly directed to attend church services. And several folks visited for long chats without managing to ask how she was feeling or what she was going through. When I inquired about this, one visitor replied, "Well I *already knew* how she felt from reading your email updates on her condition." This was from a cleric.

Right at Valerie's memorial service I was earnestly counseled to suppress negative emotion; I should get out there and *live* because "life is for the living." Several others—seeing me as a Buddhist teacher who should be well beyond worldly things—were openly disappointed to see me in grief. I felt a bit sad to disappoint them . . . and aggravated to find myself under such expectation.

It is natural that we look for ways to help. We pick up folk wisdom, psychological theories, religious faith. We hope these human tools will be useful. The problem is that, in fear, we clutch at them and impose them on others. As though a map handed down from our grandparents, if followed faithfully, could guide us through the whitewater of this moment.

The map is not the territory. *Who is here with you in this room, right now?* You don't know, but you can ask. To practice is to approach each moment with kindness and curiosity, with humor and a dignified humility. The truth is that we don't know each other's hearts.

With Valerie safely beyond all pain, and recognizing how often I make just such mistakes, it was easy to forgive everyone. And then, after a while, to see that there is nothing to forgive. And even to be grateful. Each of these friends was sincere. No one meant harm. They offered what they had to give, truly hoping it might help. They were each in real difficulty, panicked at facing death.

And, in a certain way, they misunderstood what is at stake. The Dalai Lama writes:

> When I look out at an audience, I see that all these tens of thousands of people are thinking "I," "I," "I," "I," in a way that in fact is mistaken, drawing them into trouble. Seeing them this way helps me—and will help you—call forth loving concern.

Leaning In

One can fall into a hellish state. I did. For a while, I identified with my pain, taking it as my actual self—a self cut off from the rest of the world.

This is one extreme; denial is the other. Lots of folks have religions, or personal philosophies, or family cultures that demand they stuff it down and suck it up. There is a commandment—often more powerful for not being written: *Thou shalt not feel bad.* Only losers are sad. It is just so selfish and so inconsiderate of you to be miserable.

And then, when grief hits like a bulldozer, you not only feel horrible but you feel really horrible about yourself for feeling so horrible, and then maybe even more horrible about that. It's a bad loop.

Pema Chödrön's popular book *When Things Fall Apart* elaborates on her teacher's guidance: "Lean into the sharp points." She encourages us to drop our defenses and pretenses, to head right at what terrifies us. Catastrophe, she teaches, is a precious—and too often wasted—opportunity to see into our groundlessness, the openness of our basic nature.

Such advice correctly directs us away from our biggest problem: unwillingness to face reality. In the long run, pushing emotional pain down does not help. As best we can, we need to let it in. It will stalk us until we are ready to turn around and get acquainted.

Pema Chödrön relates how this worked after her husband abruptly ended their marriage:

> When anyone asks me how I got involved with Buddhism, I always say it was because I was so angry with my husband. The truth is that he saved my life. Instinctively I knew that the annihilation of my old dependent, clinging self was the only way to go. Things are always in transition . . . Nothing ever sums itself up in the way we like to dream about. The off-center, in-between state is an ideal situation.

As with Pema Chödrön and her divorce, many survivors of traumatic loss fervently testify that cancer, blindness, or paralysis was paradoxically "the best thing that ever happened" to them. Likewise, Pema Chödrön advises:

> Death is painful and delightful. Everything that

ends is also the beginning of something else. Our whole world falls apart and we've been given this wonderful opportunity.

She invites us to celebrate our most painful losses as ideal situations. Should Valerie have been appreciative for the wonderful opportunity to have cancer? And in what sense was her death delightful?

I cannot be grateful for Valerie's death when I would so much rather it not have happened. Having felt some sharp points, I won't tell others to lean into them. To see clearly that they are sharp, to appreciate in what particular ways they are painful—this is already very hard. And then to see that they are not *my* sharp points but the condition of the world: this is sufficient.

When we go farther—when we set up gratitude for loss as a norm or an ideal—we encourage false consciousness, self-deception. Robert Aitken points at this:

> Raven said, "What if the forest burned down?"
> Wolverine said, "I might feel liberated."
> Raven bowed his head and murmured, "Oh, well . . . congratulations."

We may regard our losses as we wish, but will we also counsel Issa to celebrate his daughter's smallpox as an amazing spiritual opportunity? It is better that we join him in his sorrow, to liberate him to join us in ours.

Terrible loss is undeniably terrible. It is true that

Valerie's death opened a new phase in my life. The future, which had seemed a comfortable continuation of the past, became trackless. One could say open, like the sky. And it is true that, in this open space, I have come to see things in a new way. But when her body is burnt to ash, this is a very hard fact. It is just how things are. It doesn't help to have someone try to persuade me to regard it as a wondrous stroke of good fortune.

Barbara Ehrenreich—sick with breast cancer—deplores the norms she finds in the support community: That you must be cheerful and accepting. *That you should consider your cancer a gift.* And that if you do not adopt these celebratory attitudes, you will not recover. Olivia Newton-John spoke of what she called her "journey through cancer":

> I see it as a gift. I know it sounds strange. But I don't think I would have grown in the areas I did without this experience.

Likewise, Greg Anderson's book *Cancer: 50 Essential Things to Do* urges readers: "Seek the gift in cancer. It's there." Hearing this again and again, Ehrenreich is outraged. And I think for good reason. The power of positive thinking invalidates her distress and thereby makes it worse.

This cancer-as-gift culture is the latest phase in a long tradition running through Christian Science, New Thought, Norman Vincent Peale, and Joel Osteen. One sees its influence in every aspect of American culture, including American Buddhism. Those who gain insight after traumatic life events are entitled to this point of view. It seems to help some people feel better by finding meaning in their worst moments.

But to me it seems that they are grateful not for their losses, but for their subsequent growth. And since so many suffer trauma without such growth, I think it's important to be precise.

In any case, let's not pressure those deep in darkness to look at the bright side.

Tsunami Surfer

Something good we get from Pema Chödrön and other American Buddhist teachers is guidance toward a radical openness to our feelings—even malice and violent sorrow—so that we are not driven mindlessly by what we have suppressed. They encourage us to allow fully into consciousness all emotions, even those of which we are deeply ashamed: self-pity, rage, vengefulness, envy, self-loathing. Each has something important to tell us if we can bear to listen. This is critically important. The *Gospel of Thomas* says:

> If you bring forth what is within you, what you
> bring forth will save you. If you do not bring
> forth what is within you, what you do not bring
> forth will destroy you.

Nonetheless, without coddling oneself, sometimes it is

much more helpful to do other practices to *counteract* painful emotions. How many of us will be ready to welcome an erupting emotional volcano? A Dharma friend with an utterly horrific trauma history told me of being advised by his therapist to "express his feelings." He warned her that this was something no one would want to see. Yet.

Dr. Buddha prescribed mindful attention, but he was not a quack with just one medicine for every person in every situation. Often he specifically instructed his followers to direct their attention to particular objects so as to displace, soothe, suppress, or weaken difficult emotions. For laziness, there is the certainty of death and the uncertainty of when we will die. For agitated thoughts, focus on the breath. For anger, consider carefully the negative consequences of acting on anger. And cultivate loving-kindness. Susan Bauer-Wu describes a way to find this balance:

> If your pain really is acute then . . . other methods of dealing with such intensity may be appropriate. When . . . it is not at that kind of acuity, you have the power to investigate it with mindful awareness.

When Valerie was sick, and as she was dying, I practiced mindfulness of whatever was arising in experience, riding the waves of feeling. But sometimes I was a surfer heading right into a tsunami. I needed other practices. Then, the week after Valerie died, I formed the notion that I should clean out her purse. I did it, but it set my mind reeling in chaos. It was too soon. I was overwhelmed and utterly groundless, as though helplessly lost at sea. And I did not take this particular sense of groundlessness to be a deep insight into my basic nature.

It helps to do what we can do to turn toward reality, or to prepare to turn. We can be tender with our wounds but unafraid to face up when it is time. We can be on the lookout for the moment when a bit more becomes possible. We try to find, for ourselves and others, what is *actually helpful* in each situation. It doesn't matter where it comes from. Open awareness, or meditation on groundlessness, is not always the best practice. Meditation on emptiness is the best medicine for some but poison for those not ready.

When I could not stay with bare mindfulness, I practiced loving-kindness meditation. This was powerful and healing. In the face of grave illness and death, I had trouble with the usual phrases, "May I be well" and so on. I used the phrase "May my mind be peaceful and clear, focused and kind." And then I extended this thought to Valerie, and to Gabe, and to Becca, and then to others, and then to everyone.

In the worst moments, I could not manage even to practice loving-kindness because it requires more mental focus than I could manage. I said the Tara mantra, just to soften my mind. It is soothing to offer the mind something non-painful: *Om tare tuttare ture soha*. Then, after a while, I could return to mindfulness.

Is Hell Other People?

Eight months after Valerie died, I spoke publicly about grief to some Dharma groups. Many responded, almost immediately, by offering me details of their personal losses and traumas. These kindhearted folks had harrowing stories of childhood rape, physical abuse, and terrible loss. One had watched a childhood friend sink under quicksand and then, upon reporting this to a parent, was slapped for lying.

Naively, I had not expected this response. I had come to talk about my experience, not to hear about theirs! I felt myself pulling away. These things were hard to hear. But listening to these people and looking into their eyes, it dawned on me that I had been pitying myself. And the very moment I noticed this, I felt self-pity melting away. It was a turning point; the concussion-like haze began to lift.

The next month a colleague quoted to me a line from Sartre's *No Exit*: "Hell is other people." But I thought: that really does not sound right. Maybe hell is the self? Another half-truth.

Self is the basis for practice. Recognition of self and caring for self—self-grasping and self-cherishing—are what the path transforms. The thought of self, "I, I, I," is the source of terrible misery—but also the amazing raw material of awakening.

Other people—other living beings—are not hell. They

are the very heart of our practice. Their harmful behavior is a training ground; their pain is a training ground; their neediness is a training ground. Their otherness makes us afraid—we fear it will destroy the private sense of "I" at which we grasp. But clinging to this private sense of self leaves us alone, alienated.

Others *seem* to be hell because training is hard. Taking others seriously goes against the grain. It is hard to take fully into account their pain, their perspectives and priorities, because unlike my own, they are not self-evident to *me*.

But hell is not other people; *hell is the self turned in on itself*, unable to open and connect. This was my experience. Milton's Satan says, "Which way I fly is Hell; myself am Hell." Yes.

The fruit of practice is an unclenching, an easing of the heart into moments where self/other does not come under consideration; there is only skillful responsiveness to anguish.

Always, even now, our lives may have such grace notes: when we say something apt that we did not know we knew, when we simply help without wondering whom we are helping and why we really should. If a child is hurt, does it matter whose child?

Soko Morinaga presents it this way:

> There is no clump called "I" moving from this spot to that spot, instant by instant. Rather,

> through particular encounters with particular
> people, within each encounter, something called
> "I" makes its appearance. The heart is not an
> individual possession. Its flickering life is the
> sparkling appearance and disappearance of a
> fusion of self and its surroundings.

We never have, but only imagine, a rock-bottom foundation in our bodies or minds or *even in our most precious relationships*. We are empty and open and clear and spacious, all the way down. We are utterly free of anything frozen and hard, such as an eternal soul. Being wide open, there is natural intimacy with the world, which is empty and clear, free of divine overlords.

How to Help

So, then, how is this intimacy expressed when someone breaks her neck, or loses a limb, or is dying? Or loses his partner? How can we help those who are grieving or traumatized?

First, form a genuine and specific intention to help. When you hear of and are moved by a report of someone's suffering, make a mental commitment: "I will do something to help." Most often, we don't get even this far. We stop with "I feel for that person" or "I *should* feel for that person."

Don't fall for the illusion that this is something apart

from you. You are dying. You are facing grave loss. Joan Halifax writes:

> We may take care of a dying friend and make the natural mistake of thinking ourselves separate from her experience. In our minds, we may divide ourselves from her: "She is dying; I am the caregiver." But in reality, we are joined by the bonds of impermanence.

Don't miss a chance to be kind. See if you can say something heartfelt in a card, or an email, or face-to-face. It is natural that you may not know what to say, or fear you will say something wrong. Do the best you can. Sometimes, when you start to write, your heart opens and words appear. Most of the condolence cards I got seemed in the moment to give me no comfort. But over time they softened my sense of alienation. They connected me to people who cared for Valerie and shared, in some measure, my loss. Eventually, it dawned on me: it would have been so much worse if no one had made this gesture.

We are all busy, which means *stressed*. But I wonder: When I ask a grieving person how she is doing when I randomly bump into her in the soup aisle—does this really help? I sensed that some people asked me "How are you?" in passing so they could check it off a mental list: I was a good person today—I asked the widower how he is doing. But what can I tell you? You seem to be asking only because you misfortunately met me in the soup aisle. As C. S. Lewis observes:

> An odd by-product of my loss is that I'm afraid of being an embarrassment to everyone I meet. At work, at the club, in the street, I see people, as they approach me, trying to make up their minds whether they'll "say something about it" or not. I hate it if they do, and if they don't . . . Perhaps the bereaved ought to be isolated in special settlements like lepers.

Family survivors radiate death pollution and we are made to know this. Our presence always creates an awkward situation. We bear contagion because to face us is to face the unthinkable. We turn conversation in a terrifying direction. You know that those whom you love dearly are human. You know that all humans are mortal. But you find yourself resenting those who starkly—rudely—illustrate the inescapable conclusion. I found myself sharing C. S. Lewis's intuition:

> Whenever I meet a happily married pair, I can feel both of them thinking, "One or the other of us must some day be as he is now."

Just a week after Valerie died, Gabe, Becca, and I were invited to dinner with a group of our closest friends. There was something odd in the air: throughout the evening, no one made any mention of Valerie or what had just happened. We left early, numb. These folks later apologized for their avoidant behavior. They volunteered that, in their minds, it was important *not to remind us* of something so painful. But of course there was no such danger. We couldn't forget long enough to sleep more than a few hours.

And recently I heard this story: Five days after a woman's son died, she joined a group of friends in a knitting circle. The friends had decided, as a gift to her, to make no mention of her son's death so that she could have "a normal day." But could she have such a day?

After his wife had three miscarriages, Facebook CEO Mark Zuckerberg wrote:

> Most people don't discuss miscarriages because you worry your problems will distance you or reflect upon you—as if you're defective or did something to cause this. So you struggle on your own . . . Discussing these issues doesn't distance us; it brings us together. It creates understanding and tolerance and it gives us hope.

Don't force kindness on someone who wants to be left alone. But even if you are not very close to the grieving person, it is usually better to say something than not. We must *in some way* acknowledge that something important has happened.

When Valerie died, a few friends—fine company in fair

weather—vanished. One person, otherwise a model of kindness, ignored me for four months. When we chanced to cross paths, she promised to email so that we could get together and really talk. I never heard from her until five months later when we met again, another unhappy happenstance. And I felt terror still lurking, right below the surface of her social chatter.

In different ways, mortal terror affects us all. So when you encounter someone who has suffered trauma or loss, watch what feelings arise. Is there subtle dread or aversion? Are you pulling back or wanting to sidle away? Notice these feelings and let them flow by; open your heart.

Be wary about giving the newly bereaved false assurance that it is somehow for the best. I think it is ill-advised to tell them that this loss is an amazing spiritual opportunity. And don't notify them that they will "get over it," or that things will be OK. Usually this kind of counsel works only to manage your own fear. Sheryl Sandberg writes:

> A friend of mine with late-stage cancer told me that the worst thing people could say to him was "It is going to be okay." That voice in his head would scream, "How do you know it is going to be okay?" Real empathy is sometimes not insisting that it will be okay but acknowledging that it is not.

Rather than "How are you?" Sandberg suggests we ask, "How are you feeling today?" This implies actual, specific interest. It implies sensitivity to painful feelings and awareness that they are constantly changing.

Perhaps say how deeply sorry you are to hear of the person's loss. If you are able, offer something specific, factual, and from the heart about the deceased. Can you recall some particular kindness that the deceased showed? When people were able to do this, I found it helpful.

If your relationship with a grieving person allows, look for situations where she can share feelings, or tell and retell the stories. It might feel right to say: "I can't imagine what you are going through. I have had grief in my life, but I am really wondering what this could be like for you."

Or just to be together in intimate silence. Halifax, in her hospice work, asks herself:

> What words will benefit her? Does anything really need to be said? Can I relax and trust in simply being here, without needing my personality to mediate the tender connection we share?

From within the nakedness of not knowing, *bearing witness* means giving full and open attention. Such attention is to the heart what light and water are to a wounded tree. It is rare because it is hard to give. It demands not deflecting back to yourself or to something *so similar* that happened to your grandmother. It demands not turning away in the presence of what terrifies us, and not trying to make it all right, even when everyone so wishes that it were.

When we meet someone who is truly competent to listen, we may find that we are ready to talk about things that we have never admitted to ourselves. The traumatized are often more able to talk with those whom they identify as having had a similar loss. For example, combat vets can't explain the inexplicable to the rest of us.

I felt best talking to Grayson, a friend whose wife died of brain cancer, leaving him with two adolescents. We could talk honestly and laugh about our common problems. What to do with all that Tupperware? How many casseroles and lasagnas are in your freezer? Joyce Carol Oates recounts her desolation amid the condolence debris:

> Why are people sending me these things? Do they imagine that grief will be assuaged by chocolate-covered truffles, pâté de foie gras, pepperoni sausage? Do they imagine assistants shield me from the labor of dealing with such a quantity of trash? I am frantic to get rid of this party food—I am infuriated, disgusted, ashamed—for of course I should be grateful.

It is easier to give a mountain of food than to have a real conversation.

Since each grief and trauma is different, we cannot always be the very best person to help . . . but maybe we know of someone who is. Hearing about grief experiences that were like mine, or worse, was helpful in the beginning because it stopped my fear about my mental state—the shivering and the inability to concentrate. And hearing about others' grief and trauma was even more healing later because it dissolved my self-pity and hellish alienation.

Seeing others' pain, and feeling that we just might be able to ease it in some way—often this is the best therapy for our wounds. Some of Valerie's last visitors came, without even realizing it, to get off-the-books therapy from the dying woman. And she helped them. And this helped her.

I did feel put-upon when, within a month of Valerie's death, people pressed me to give talks, to help with scholarly problems, and to assume leadership roles. But those who imposed upon me in this way, forbearing my negative mindset, gave me the chance to become helpful and were therefore great helpers.

What Did the Buddha Do?

When the monk Tissa was dying, he could not take care of himself; he was alone in squalid conditions. Seeing this, the Buddha went to Tissa. He bathed him and dressed him in clean clothes and sat with him as he died. Then the Buddha told the other monks that they must always care for one another in this way. If we do not care for one another, then who will?

Years later, the Buddha knew that his time was at hand. He told his follower and friend Ananda, and Ananda was distressed. The Buddha calmly reminded him of his teachings on impermanence. It was a gentle reminder: "What have I been telling you, after all?" One might take it that the Buddha's death was the culmination of his teaching, a skillful demonstration to awaken others. As a monk who had heard the Dharma for many years, this was the kind of medicine Ananda needed.

But when helping those less well prepared and in the midst of grief-trauma, the Buddha took a subtler approach. The famous story of Kisa Gotami illustrates how it may be unhelpful to tell the grief-stricken to suck it up and get on with their lives. And it offers a compassionate alternative.

Kisa Gotami, "Skinny Gotami," was from a poor family. She married a higher status man and her in-laws looked on her with scorn. But she gave birth to a son, precious to her and making her precious to her in-laws. Unfortunately, the young boy died after an accidental fall while playing. Seized by psychotic grief, she carried her son's corpse around the town, begging for medicine. "Are you crazy?" people said. "He's dead!" She was carrying around a corpse, a source of horrific pollution. But one man compassionately sent her to see the Buddha.

Kisa Gotami pleaded with the Buddha for his help. And, seeing her mental state clearly, he answered: "I can help you, but you have to get me mustard seed from a household where no one has ever died."

Mustard seed was common, the cheapest sort of spice. So when she went door to door everyone had it—but there were no families where no one had died. Every time she knocked on a door, she heard another hard story. Every house was bereaved. Repeatedly looking into the eyes of others who had borne terrible pain, her heart unclenched. Looking down on the town at the end of the day, she knew the pervasiveness of loss. One thousand doses of empathy purged Kisa Gotami of her psychotic grief.

All over Asia, the Buddhist tradition is especially linked to funerals, death, and impermanence. But the Buddha did not preach at Kisa Gotami; he guided her skillfully. There are lots of true things one can say—but which will be kind and helpful?

Who knows? We are not omniscient buddhas. We are not clairvoyant—the truth is that we actually don't know which words, or what kind of silence, will help most. We can start by knowing that we don't know. And from within that not-knowing, we can offer our presence, our fullest effort and attention. We can aspire to become attuned and skillful caregivers. We act, as best we can, so as to be most helpful in each distinct situation.

When we set out to meditate on our breath, we soon become distracted; the practice is to notice this and return to the breath. Our care for others likewise progresses in error and recommitment. Be prepared: we, the well inten- tioned, will soon say or do exactly the wrong thing. Mean- ing to help, we will sometimes make things worse. Let's acknowledge that, forgive ourselves, try again.

We think, "I cannot bear my own losses, so how can I be intimate with others' private pain?" And so, drawing a false and rigid boundary, we turn back the best medicine.

When I spoke about grief, and heard in return of others' pain, it was clear: Kisa Gotami's story is in some modest way my own.

And of course, it cannot be mine in particular.

Perhaps it is, or will be, your story as well.

Eulogy

Have you personally met anyone who truly inspired you?
Who might that be?

In 1990, someone asked me this and I gave the truest
answer I could find: *No.* But there was a haze of doubt.
That doubt swelled and revealed its source: five years
before, in the same year, I had met the Dalai Lama—and
married Valerie.

The fourth time Valerie's sister Kay got married, she
notified us via voicemail a few days after the wedding. We
called back to wish Kay better luck this time. Her latest
ex was in prison for poaching—on a college campus. And
also hijacking his neighbor's fishing boat. While awaiting
trial, Walmart nabbed him loading an unpurchased lawn
tractor into his truck.

Kay's other sister missed the wedding too. She was
doing five years "to the door" (no early release) for eighth-
offense shoplifting.

Then, the autumn Valerie got her metastatic diagnosis,

Kay's son hanged himself from a tree in his grandmother's yard. He was a crack addict in despair. Valerie's mother went out to rake leaves and found the corpse. So . . . that is something about her family.

We humans tell stories. Our animal bodies survive on bread, but meaning sustains human life. We weave dream worlds of meaning from story and gesture, song and rhythm. A few of us aspire to plunge into the heart of the great matter, to scrabble right down past all words to the *thing itself*. But when we surface, we tell the story—it would be mean-spirited not to do so. And thus it is well that we know it as a story. Perhaps it can point the way.

We know some great Dalai Lama stories. Here is a story about another healer—one who worked on a smaller scale.

Becoming a Person

When asked, "Is there a way for a person to live?" the master Dongshan replied, "When you become a person, there will be."

Valerie Lynne Stephens was born in Atlanta, raised in Miami, found friends and an education in the public universities of Virginia; she built a career and raised her family in central Michigan. She became many things to many people—therapist, friend, wife, mother, and business owner; world traveler, film buff, Dostoevsky fan, and inspired cook.

But none of these passions and powers was a birthright or ready inheritance. Valerie worked hard, with enthusiasm and discipline, throughout her life. And she worked with her head up, looking to what more might be possible. With meticulous attention, with integrity and rugged persistence, she put it all together. She made all the connections she needed to grow into a caring, powerful, and complex person.

Valerie's mother, Gladys, is the daughter of subsistence tenant farmers from the red clay at the south end of Appalachia. Valerie's father was a cruel sociopath who terrorized his family in fits of rage. Once he took his wife and young kids for a summer boat trip in the Atlantic—and then abandoned them on a small, sandy island. Another time, he chased Valerie down and beat her with a boat oar.

When Valerie was in middle school, her father tried to murder a young man whom he suspected of being her boyfriend. Valerie witnessed her friend's narrow escape from death. Her father kept the family constantly on the run, one step ahead of the blowback from his schemes . . . so Valerie could not say where she was "from."

This isn't the whole story. There never is one—there is always more and always another version. But it is enough to see why Valerie felt that she was in the wrong clan. She actually clawed through her mother's closet hunting adoption papers. Her heart told her that this could not be her whole world.

And so she set out to explore, at first in the only way she could: by reading. She would go deep in the Georgia pines—and later, in Miami, into other people's yards—to just sit and read in peace. She pleaded with her mother to get her Nancy Drew books, and then later a set of encyclopedias. Reading was respite in realms of imagination; reading was adventure and also the start of a deep education.

But even more—and crucially—reading helped her become a person of interest and in time a person of *notable value* to certain teachers and neighbors. And through being esteemed in such relationships, she found the trailhead for the path to becoming the person I knew.

Easing Pain

After Valerie's last breath, sitting with her and the kids, I called her mother. We cried and after a while Gladys choked out the opening line in her version of the story: "Even as a young girl, Valerie had *a heart to help others*." She was intelligent, but beyond this she was a sort of emotional prodigy, keenly attuned to the feelings of people and animals around her. But how could she use these gifts—to make a living, to help others, to make a life?

At sixteen, Valerie was emancipated, on her own and supporting herself. Working as a behavioral technician at a state mental hospital, she noticed that those who had the greatest ability to help the residents were the clinical psychologists. So, with money from loans and part-time jobs, she graduated from the University of Virginia (with highest distinction) and went on to earn a Ph.D. in clinical psychology from Virginia Commonwealth University. Her family could not begin to fathom why she borrowed money for education. None had gone to college; many had not finished high school; some had not finished grade school.

Through years of clinical practice, and through always reading the best clinical literature, Valerie gradually gained confidence in her ability to help others. She was never content to deploy her natural talents, remarkable as they were; she was always refining her understanding and technique.

And she worked even harder to understand herself. With therapists in Virginia and later in Michigan, she traced the precise contours of her own wounds—and as she began to heal, she became more and more adept as a healer.

Valerie cared deeply for her clients and poured her whole energy into helping them. She took great satisfaction in her frequent successes. She was grateful to them for sharing their personal lives with her. She told me that a great deal of what she knew was learned directly in interaction with clients. Irretrievable now is the fine-grained quality of Valerie's insight; we could never persuade her to write a book or even to make a video.

Attachment and Balance

We do know the core themes Valerie saw emerging from her work. First, there are an enormous number of people who are badly hurt by their parents. Child abuse and neglect—and even well intentioned but misguided parenting—leave a legacy of harm that is passed through generations. Vast, needless misery could be relieved if adults had children only when well prepared. Crucially, parents should be ready to help children develop *secure attachment* through being attuned and appropriately responsive to children's emotional states.

Valerie found that some adult survivors of abuse attempt to cope, to defend themselves, by striving for constant control of what surrounds them. Often high-achievers in their careers, they run into problems in personal relationships as they try to exercise the control that they need to feel safe. At some level, they believe that bad things happened to them because they failed to control their environments when they were children. The big challenge in their lives is to achieve intimacy by allowing themselves to be vulnerable in the right relationships. This was an issue for Valerie herself.

But of course she saw many survivors of childhood abuse who went to the other extreme. As children, they learned all too well the lesson of helplessness, and so as adults find themselves stuck in passivity, depression, and sometimes revictimization. Their challenge is to find the courage to see that their choices matter, that their actions actually can make a difference.

All of us can benefit by finding balance here, recognizing that we *can* be effective in the world, but that even as adults—just as when we were children—there are sometimes tsunami-like forces that are beyond our control and for whose harmful effects we are therefore not to blame. This frees us to care for others with equanimity rather than desperation.

Valerie found many of her clients struggling to face their negative emotions. Here again, she offered guidance toward a middle way, neither denying such emotions nor wallowing in them and identifying with them. Valerie insisted that it is healthy to open our minds to emotions such as anger, fear, envy, and grief. We can take notice, realistically, of just what we are feeling here in our bodies. In this way, painful feelings can teach us without controlling our behavior. Feeling them is natural.

Our families and our culture goad us to suppress and deny difficult emotions, but the force of these feelings does not thereby vanish. Without our notice, they affect our behavior and our well-being. If we can give ourselves full permission to feel all of our feelings, and to name them, then we can learn from them and work with them. Less and less often will we find ourselves acting impulsively, driven helplessly by what we have refused to allow into the light. When we are intentional in noticing exactly how we feel anger rising in our bodies, for example, then we have a moment to reflect before we act, a chance to choose to be assertive rather than aggressive, or caring rather than cruel.

Arrayed against this mindful and balanced approach are theories, folk psychologies, family traditions, role models, and some religious teachers urging that we experience only upbeat, positive, optimistic feelings. Some go so far as to claim that *everything* good or bad in our lives is the result of our own positive or negative thoughts and emotions. Sadly, many people are thereby misled into believing that when bad things happen to someone, it is inevitably because that person somehow opened herself to negative thoughts or feelings.

Valerie was vehement in her opposition to this toxic philosophy. It causes harm both by encouraging unhealthy repression of natural feelings, such as grief and anger, and also because it blames every victim—of rape, or cancer— for failing to control, via positive mental attitudes, events that they actually could not control.

Commitment

Valerie intentionally set out to develop her particular talents into skills she could use to help others. Aware of her own wounds, she tuned in to the nuances of others' pain, becoming a powerful guide and healer.

Resilience is the courage to be loyal to our deepest nature and greatest potential, to persevere even when faced with terrible obstacles. Valerie embodied this courage.

In Japan, the beloved deceased are *hotoke*—a term that vaguely assimilates them into the buddha realm—from the viewpoint of their families. Whatever we may think of this, Valerie is like this for those who were closest to her. She reached a flourishing maturity and helped many who needed help. We take it that she has at last passed beyond pain.

She was a bodhisattva in that, working with what she had, she dedicated herself with fearless integrity to becoming the most powerful helper of others that she could become. She alleviated misery and created causes for future awakening. We can only commit ourselves to living up to what she embodied.

In a blizzard, in the coldest part of the coldest winter, two hundred people gathered for her memorial service. In closing, we recited these words together:

> May I be a protector for those in danger,
> A guide for travelers along the way.
> For those struggling in troubled waters
> May I always be like a raft
> Or a bridge to the far shore.

Valerie (center) at Western State Mental Hospital
Staunton, Virginia, circa 1973

Resources

In approaching death in any way, I particularly recommend *Being with Dying* by Joan Halifax. If you are going through a difficult grief, it might be helpful to read or skim *A Widow's Story* by Joyce Carol Oates. It came into my hands highly recommended by members of a grief support group. It helped me to see just how painful "normal grief" can be— and how, even so, it is impermanent. Most hospices have good literature on grieving and organize support groups. The website thedinnerparty.org connects young adults who have lost parents. There are other things like this and we can help there to be even more.

For each of us, there are different texts that will be most useful. Robert Aitken's *Zen Master Raven* is the thing for me, but it cannot be everyone's cup of tea. Sogyal Rinpoche's *Tibetan Book of Living and Dying* has been helpful to many. Tara Brach's *True Refuge* gives good advice on facing grave adversity. Chade-Meng Tan's *Search Inside Yourself* gives good introductory instructions on mindfulness and mindful listening. A deeper consideration of mindful listening is found at the end of chapter 11 in *Being with Dying*. Joseph Goldstein's *A Heart Full of Peace* and Sharon Salzberg's *Lovingkindness* have good instructions on meditative practices that can be helpful when dealing with strong emotions. Roz Chast's graphic memoir *Can't We Talk About Something More Pleasant?* poignantly recounts caring for parents as they age and die. Soko Morinaga's *Novice to Master* is a memoir with deep insights on facing death and overcoming fear.

Acknowledgments

I am grateful to many who supported me, including Jim Heavenrich, Scott Vogel, Chuck Blaksmith and Linda Byers-Blaksmith, Grayson Holmbeck, Risha Bale, Alan Jackson, Venerable Thubten Chodron and the Sravasti community, and my friends in the Geshe Wangyal lineage including Joshua and Diana Cutler. Thanks to Don Lopez, Betsy Napper, Anne Klein, and Dan Cozort. Thanks to David Smith and all of my colleagues at CMU. Thanks to my amazingly understanding dean, Pamela Gates. Thanks to Dick Parfitt, Bob Horan, and the gang. I much appreciate the support of the Unitarian Universalist Fellowship of Central Michigan University, including Beth MacLeod, Gisela Moffit, Liz Dealing, and Laura McBride. Thanks to my siblings—Chris Newland, Kit Newland, Scott Newland, and Jeanne Newland—and to my children, Gabe Newland and Becca Newland. And thanks to Tim McNeill and Josh Bartok at Wisdom.

Notes

Epigraph and Introduction

The epigraphs are from the *Maha-parinibbana Sutta* and *A Grief Observed*.

The notion of "pretraumatic" derives from Mark Epstein's "The Trauma of Being Alive" in *The New York Times Sunday Review*, August 3, 2013. Ven. Thubten Chodron gave me this definition of grief.

Joyce Carol Oates's *A Widow's Story* is an astonishingly vivid account of traumatic grief. Other recent and remarkable records are Joan Didion's *The Year of Magical Thinking* and Julian Barnes's *Levels of Life*.

Most of whatever Dharma I know comes from Tibetan-lineage teachers. But my personal sense of being Buddhist has kinship with Gary Snyder's *Practice of the Wild*, Jay Garfield's *Engaging Buddhism*, and Robert Aitken's *Zen Master Raven*.

The phrase "the middle of the road of life" alludes to the

opening of Dante's *Divine Comedy*, where Virgil describes his situation before beginning his tour of hell, purgatory, and heaven. The phrase "a season in hell" alludes to the poem of that title by Arthur Rimbaud.

1. Pain

Roz Chast's memoir, *Can't We Talk About Something More Pleasant?* directs our attention to the tendency to prefer any topic to the topic of death. Joyce Carol Oates describes shivering in grief many times in *A Widow's Story*, where she also uses the phrase "death duties." Joan Halifax's *Being with Dying* describes how postmortem busyness can prevent one from feeling one's feelings. Joan Didion's *The Year of Magical Thinking* cites a medical study in which grief is characterized by

> sensations of somatic distress occurring *in waves* lasting from twenty minutes to an hour at a time, a feeling of tightness in the throat, choking with shortness of breath, need for sighing, and an empty feeling in the abdomen, lack of muscular power, and an intense distress subjects described as tension or mental pain.

C. S. Lewis's *A Grief Observed* compares grief to being concussed. On the sense of having lost someone, the same text says:

> In what place is she at the present time? If H. is
> not a body—and the body that I loved is cer-
> tainly no longer she—she is in no place at all.

It also describes how, even when almost unable to function, the grieving person can still do some things through
habit:

> No one ever told me about the laziness of grief.
> Except at my job—where the machine seems
> to run on as usual—I loathe the slightest effort.
> Not only writing, but even writing a letter is too
> much. Even shaving. What does it matter now if
> my cheek is rough or smooth?

Atul Gawande's *Being Mortal* shows that across cultures,
people who expect to die sooner focus their energies more
immediately on what is truly most important to them and,
as a consequence, experience more positive emotions than
those for whom death is merely a theoretical proposition.
The passage on the charnel ground meditation is from the
Establishment of Mindfulness Sutta.

2. *Intimacy*

I rely here on the Dalai Lama's books *How to See Yourself as
You Really Are, How to Practice, From Here to Enlightenment*, and
his comments on the DVD *Compassion in Exile*. I also rely on

Jeffrey Hopkins's *The Truthful Heart*, Tsongkhapa's *Compassion in Tibetan Buddhism*, and Tsongkhapa's *Great Treatise on the Stages of the Path to Enlightenment*. The phrasing of the passage about the measure of practice being kindness derives from an oral communication with Ven. Thubten Chodron. The Pema Chödrön passage combines two sentences from different parts of *When Things Fall Apart*.

Here and throughout this book I rely on Robert Aitken's *Zen Master Raven*. In the preface to this book, Nelson Foster reports that Aitken identified this book as having come from "a deep sleep." The Dogen passage is from *Shobogenzo* as translated in *The Essential Dogen*. The lines about training as repetition in ordinary domestic tasks allude to Gary Snyder's *Practice of the Wild;* the notion that "nothing good happens fast" comes from Carroll Arnett's "The Old Man Said: One" in *Night Perimeter*.

The story of the attempt to assassinate the Buddha is in the *Cullavaga*, a section of the *Vinaya Pitaka*. The description of the Buddha's reaction to this comes from two different suttas with the same name, *The Stone Sliver Sutta*. One of these reports:

> Severe pains assailed the Blessed One—bodily feelings that were painful, racking, sharp, piercing, harrowing, disagreeable.

The phrase "mothers (and others)" alludes to *Mothers and Others* by Sarah Blaffer Hrdy. The discussion of the development of a secure basis from which to extend care is based mainly on David Wallin's *Attachment in Psychotherapy*. Wallin shows that a subgroup of secure parents had painful childhoods but "earned" security in emotionally significant relationships with friends, partners, or therapists, and through the practice of mindfulness in which they learn to recognize their mental states *as* mental states.

I cite Mary Oliver's "The Messenger" and reference George Saunders's *Congratulations, by the way: Some Thoughts on Kindness*. The notion of the importance of self-reproach comes from *Writings from the Philokalia*, a passage referenced in John Berryman's *Dream Songs*. The criteria for religious experience are from William James's *Varieties of Religious Experience*.

I do not know the source for the line about knowing the names of neighborhood dogs.

3. *The Great Matter*

Here I cite *The Blue Cliff Record* translated by Thomas Cleary and J. C. Cleary, Robert Aitken's *Zen Master Raven*, Soko Morinaga's *Novice to Master*, and Shunryu Suzuki's *Zen Mind, Beginner's Mind*, as well as "Samadhi of the Treasury of Radiant Light" from Okamura's *Living by Vow*.

That it is unhelpful to blame ourselves for being human derives from Robert Aitken's *Taking the Path of Zen*. The Blue Sky and Green Earth of One Mind is from Snyder's "Smokey the Bear Sutra." The story about Katagiri Roshi pretending to die comes from Halifax's *Being with Dying*.

Sushila Blackman's *Graceful Exits* compiles stories of

spiritual teachers dying well. The prevalence of such stories surely reflects our fear of death and our hope that spirituality will allow us to transcend it. In Dostoyevsky's *The Brothers Karamazov*, devotees of the saintly Zosima wait anxiously for a postmortem miracle. Instead, his body decays quickly with a putrid odor.

The Dalai Lama frequently points out (for example, in *From Here to Enlightenment* and *How to See Yourself As You Really Are*) that if things actually existed the way they appear to us—objectively real on their own side—then, when we analytically scrutinize them, they should get clearer rather than more elusive. This has a classical basis in Nagarjuna's *Precious Garland*, verses 52–56.

Regarding the notion that what has happened is both ineradicable and effective, Jeffrey Hopkins notes in *A Truthful Heart*:

> After the deed is done, you remain the person
> who went down one fork rather than another.

The Derek Parfit quote is part of the epigraph to *A Widow's Story*, excerpted from a message he sent Joyce Carol Oates after her husband's death.

A discussion of the effectiveness of past actions in Madhyamaka is found in Cozort's *Unique Tenets Middle Way Consequence School*. A Tibetan debate about this issue is explained in my essay "How Does Merely Conventional Karma Work?" in the Cowherds' *Moonpaths*.

Obviously, the grief-shock discussed in this book is not experienced in the same way by all. A number of long-time practitioners have told me of significant personal success in coping with the deaths of close family members by anticipating them and meditating on them regularly. Arguably, meditation on impermanence and death is anticipatory grief-work, built into Buddhist practice throughout the world. Effectiveness seems to depend on contemplating the deaths of particular beloved individuals, regularly, over a long period of time.

That the Dharma does not go with the flow is beautifully expressed by Robert Aitken in *Zen Master Raven*. That the Dharma goes against the grain is expressed in the Buddhist tradition by the term *pratiloma*, which suggests pulling hair opposite to the way it grows. Stephen Batchelor's *Buddhism Without Beliefs* articulates the view that actual Dharma is never about consolation. In this part, I cite Pema Chödrön's *When Things Fall Apart* and Donald Lopez's *The Scientific Buddha*.

The discussion of what happens to awakened persons at the end of their last lifetime refers to several short suttas: the *Vaccagotta Sutta*, the *Vaccagotta on Fire Sutta*, the *Ananda Sutta*, and the *Anuradha Sutta*. In the last of these, the Buddha says:

> You can't pin down the Tathagata even in the present life.

The Zen parallel to this is in the *Gateless Gate*, where Bodhidharma's future successor asks Bodhidharma to pacify his mind. Bodhidharma says: "If you bring me that mind, I will pacify it for you." The successor says: "When I search my mind I cannot hold it." Bodhidharma says: "Then your mind is pacified already."

The idea that understanding requires deep attention to whatever presents itself, rather than turning the mind to some alternate reality, references Tsongkhapa's *Great Treatise on the Stages of the Path* and Jeffrey Hopkins's *Emptiness Yoga*.

The story about Ajahn Chah comes from "Already Broken," a sermon by James Ishmael Ford available at: uubf.org/docs/sermons/sermon3.htm. The Chuang Tzu (or Zhuangzi) passage is from Burton Watson's translation in *Selected Writings*. I cite Thoreau's *Walden* and Susan Bauer-Wu at www.mindful.org/susan-bauer-wu-mindfulness-and-coping-with-pain/. The reference to Issa is from Nobuyaki Yuasa's translation of *The Year of My Life*. The Tolstoy passage is from "The Death of Ivan Ilyich."

In a 1923 letter to Nanny von Escher (*Briefe aus Muzot: 1921 bis 1926*), Rainer Maria Rilke confides:

> Two inner experiences were necessary for the creation of these books [*The Sonnets to Orpheus* and *The Duino Elegies*]. One is the increasingly conscious decision to hold life open to death. The other is the spiritual imperative to present, in this wider context, the transformations of

love that are not possible in a narrower circle
where Death is simply excluded as the Other.

The Nagarjuna passage is my free translation collapsing
verses 63 and 73 from *Essay on the Mind of Awakening*, a text
attributed to Nagarjuna. In *From Here to Enlightenment*, the
Dalai Lama mentions that both Nagarjuna and Haribhadra
state that "attachment" to the welfare of others is a result
of meditation on emptiness.

4. Karma

The first part of this chapter is based on a paper offered
at the University of Virginia in celebration of the career
of Jeffrey Hopkins, upon his retirement, April 20, 2005.
Relevant information can be found at www.nytimes.com
/2012/12/05/sports/basketball/rasheed-wallace-keeps-
technicals-fouls-flowing-with-ball-dont-lie.html.

The Geertz verse is from *The Interpretation of Cultures*. The
discussion of how religions offer consolation by confirm-
ing our original, naive hopes derives from my book *The
Two Truths*. The *Precious Garland* and *Samadhiraja Sutra* pas-
sages are drawn from *The Great Treatise on the Stages of the Path
to Enlightenment*. On the theme that we reap what we sow in
the Bible, see Job 4:8, Jeremiah 17:10, Hosea 10:12–13,
and the letters of Paul, especially Galatians 6:7 and 2 Cor-
inthians 9:6.

The phrase "It's a fact that we all get whacked," comes
to us via Dan Cozort. Dan suffered life-altering injuries

when a car hit his bicycle. Shortly after that, a friend of his used this phrase.

I cite Nobuyuki Yuasa's translation of Issa's *The Year of My Life*. The Melvill quote is from the sermon on "Partaking in Other Men's Sins" as it appears in *The Golden Lectures*. I quote Pema Chödrön from *When Things Fall Apart* and Soko Morinaga from *Novice to Master*.

On the notion that we would rather feel guilty than helpless, Elaine Pagels poignantly discusses this with reference to her experience with a terminally ill child. See part 2 of an interview about her book *Adam, Eve, and the Serpent* with Bill Moyers on *A World of Ideas*. This is available at www.vimeo.com/33300564.

On the supposed bad karma of Jewish Holocaust victims, I refer to Loy's *Money, Sex, War, Karma*. Loy comments:

> This kind of fundamentalism, which blames the victims and rationalizes their horrific fate, is something no longer to be tolerated quietly. It is time for modern Buddhists and modern Buddhism to outgrow it by accepting social responsibility and finding ways to address such injustices.

The sutta passage suggesting that it is wrong to hold that all we experience is the result of our karma is from the *Sutta Nipata*, slightly adapted for clarity from the full citation in Loy's *Money, Sex, War, Karma*.

Nagarjuna's warning about the danger of misunderstanding emptiness refers to chapter 24 of his *Fundamental*

Treatise on the Middle Way, especially verse 11. The idea that the meaning of emptiness is dependent-arising is the same chapter, verse 18.

On the problem of sutras contradicting one another, the Dalai Lama's *From Here to Enlightenment* says:

> When it comes to determining which sutra is definitive, we cannot rely entirely on scripture because . . . the scriptures seem to contradict one another . . . In fact, the only way we can differentiate the definitive [sutras] is by means of reasoning and analysis.

A very short summary of recent scholarship on karma is found at the end of "How Does Merely Conventional Karma Work," a chapter of the Cowherds' *Moonpaths*. The Tibetan tradition considers the workings of karma "extremely hidden" so as to be comprehensible only to a buddha. In the *Anguttara Nikaya*, the Buddha says that pondering the fruition of karma will lead to insanity.

On the hollowness of finding consolation in claims that the universe is fair, Stephen Batchelor's *Buddhism Without Beliefs* argues that we should look to the Dharma "for metaphors of existential confrontation rather than metaphors of existential consolation." He argues that anguish is rooted in craving that seeks consolation in something permanent and reliable, such as a God in charge of destiny or a controlling self. He further argues that we cling to moral certainty that is at odds with a changing world because this is consoling and blunts "awareness of the uniqueness of each ethical moment."

5. Taking Care

On not knowing, bearing witness, and compassionate action, Halifax's *Being with Dying* attributes this framework to her teacher, Bernie Glassman. The notion of not knowing as a kind of wisdom has a long history in Zen and its precursors. I quote Lao Tzu (Laozi) from the translation by Giu-Fu Feng and Joan English. The Susan Bauer-Wu passage is from www.mindful.org/susan -bauer-wu-mindfulness-and-coping-with-pain/.

Elisabeth Kübler-Ross's book *On Death and Dying* broke open this topic in the United States. This and her subsequent work famously use a classification of grieving in five stages: denial, anger, bargaining, depression, and acceptance. Several relatives of dying persons have told me that the simplistic and mechanical application of this schema by clerics, nurses, and others has been counterproductive and in some cases infuriating. Considerable subsequent research on grieving has brought appropriate nuance and complexity to the matter. For example, see the 2007 article by Paul Maciejewski, Baohui Zhang, Susan Block, and Holly Prigerson, "An Empirical Examination of the Stage Theory of Grief," in *The Journal of the American Medical Association*.

In this chapter, I quote Shunryu Suzuki's *Zen Mind, Beginner's Mind*, Pema Chödrön's *When Things Fall Apart*, Robert

Aitken's *Zen Master Raven*, Soko Morinaga's *Novice to Master*, the Dalai Lama's *How To See Yourself As You Really Are*, C. S. Lewis's *A Grief Observed*, and Joyce Carol Oates's *A Widow's Story*. Some of these quotes have ellipses, left unmarked for the sake of readability.

The *Gospel of Thomas* is an early collection of sayings attributed to Jesus. It did not become part of the Christian Bible but has become widely available since being rediscovered in 1945.

I quote Greg Anderson's *Cancer: 50 Essential Things To Do*. Barbara Ehrenreich's book on mandatory positivity in cancer culture is *Bright-Sided*. Another very readable critique of positive thinking is Oliver Burkeman's *The Antidote*.

The syllogism that begins, "You know that those whom you love . . . " alludes to the passage about Caius in Leo Tolstoy's "The Death of Ivan Ilyich."

As social beings, with mirror neurons functioning, we often have intuitions about the inner landscape of others. However, as Nicholas Epley's *Mindwise* shows, we also have a tendency to overestimate how well we know what others are thinking and feeling.

The phrase "the map is not the territory" derives from the semantics work of Alfred Korzybski. Jonathan Z. Smith brought it more light in his book *Map Is Not Territory*.

On the notion of an unwritten commandment not to feel bad, the Christian conception has been that sadness is either a direct consequence of sin or an indirect consequence of the original sin of the Fall. On this orthodoxy and Julian's alternative to it, see Elaine Pagels's *Adam, Eve, and the Serpent.* Pope Gregory (d. 604) listed sadness (*tristia*) as one of the seven principal vices (*Moralia in Job*). Later lists of seven cardinal sins or seven deadly sins, such as that in Thomas Aquinas's *On Evil*, do not count sadness as a separate sin, but incorporate it into the sin of sloth or spiritual apathy (*acedia*).

On working with anger, see *Working With Anger* by Thubten Chodron. Chapters 2 and 16 deal with the approaches I mention here, but she has a great many useful insights. Other important insights are found in chapter 8 of Harvey Aronson's *Buddhist Practice on Western Ground*.

On groundlessness, it is a concern that some might assume that any mental state characterized by derealization or depersonalization constitutes insight into the profound. For example, see: www.theguardian.com/society/2014/aug/25/mental-health-meditation.

The claim that ordinary beings can have direct experiences of our fundamental nature is controversial and is subject to extensive critique in Tsongkhapa's *Great Treatise on the Stages of the Path to Enlightenment*. For example, Tsongkhapa argues that diaphanous, hazy, rainbow-like appearances that arise through stabilizing the mind nondiscursively do not constitute insight into the illusion-like nature of phenomena unless they are directly supported by profound insight into things' lack of intrinsic nature.

C. S. Lewis touches on the issue of self-pity at the outset of *A Grief Observed*.

Jean-Paul Sartre's play *Huis Clos* includes the line, "L'enfer, c'est les autres." Sartre seems to intend this in a specific sense that I am not directly engaging here; I am using the bare words as a starting point for my own reflection. The Milton passage is from *Paradise Lost, The Fourth Book.*

On children being hurt: In the 2005 film *The Girl in the Café,* Lawrence asks Gina why she was in prison.

> Gina: I hurt a man.
> Lawrence: Why?
> Gina: Because he hurt a child . . . killed a child.
> Lawrence: Your child?
> Gina: Does it matter whose child?

On small moments of awakening within ordinary life, when we say something we did not know we knew, I draw from Batchelor's *Buddhism Without Beliefs.*

The Zuckerberg quote is from a 7/31/2015 post on his Facebook page (www.facebook.com/zuck). On things being open and clear to the very bottom, in *Zen Master Raven* Porcupine—who will eventually succeed Raven as roshi—reports:

> Last night when I was putting little Porky to bed, I suddenly realized that everything is open and clear to the very bottom.

On how some friends' fear of death is such that they cannot face a grieving person, *A Grief Observed* comments:

Some funk it altogether. R. has been avoiding me for a week.

The Sandberg quote and the idea of saying "How are you today?" comes from Sheryl Sandberg's Facebook post after the death of her husband:

> Even a simple "How are you?"—almost always asked with the best of intentions—is better replaced with "How are you today?" When I am asked "How are you?" I stop myself from shouting, My husband died a month ago, how do you think I am? When I hear "How are you today?" I realize the person knows that the best I can do right now is to get through each day.

The story of the Buddha's helping Tissa appears in Halifax's *Being with Dying*. The *Commentary to the Dhammapada* seems to be the main source for this story. Also, in the *Monk with Dysentery* (*Kucchivikara-vatthu*), the Buddha comes to the assistance of a sick monk whom the other monks had not been caring for. He then instructs the monks:

> Monks, you have no mother, you have no father, who might tend to you. If you don't tend to one another, who then will tend to you? Whoever would tend to me, should tend to the sick.

On the Buddha's teaching to Ananda, the *Maha-parinibbana Sutta* reports the Buddha saying to Ananda:

> It is nothing strange that human beings should die.

When he later announces to Ananda that he has renounced his will to live, Ananda pleads with him to remain. When the monks are assembled, he exhorts them:

> All compounded things are subject to vanish.
> Strive with earnestness.

This Kisa Gotami story is found in the commentary to the *Verses of the Elder Nuns* (*Therigatha*). In retelling it, I draw the inference that many of the townspeople would naturally tell their grief stories to Kisa. After teaching Kisa's story one time, I was startled to find this composed in my mind the next morning:

Real Estate

bullet-hole (?), bloodstain, burn-mark,
the bones of long-loved pets
forgotten under the yard,
every home is the site of violence
fear, pain, death and grief—
the only exception is the empty house
where no one has ever lived.

Emphasis on the inevitability of saying or doing the wrong thing derives from a private communication with the Ven. Thubten Chodron. As I have given talks based on the material in this book, I have found that things I say here—while helpful to some—are the wrong medicine for others.

Eulogy

On scrabbling down to the thing itself, I allude to "Diving into the Wreck" by Adrienne Rich and also to John Berryman's "Dream Song #384."

"Is there a way for a person to live?" is attributed to Dong-shan in Gary Snyder's *Practice of the Wild*. My comment on resilience is adapted from online comments by Larry Glover. For example, www.academia.edu/4264085/Call_of_the_Wild_Resiliency_Within.

David Wallin's *Attachment in Psychotherapy* was one of Valerie's favorite books. Growing up white in the South, the first book that reshaped her understanding of the world was *The Learning Tree*. She died in the midst of reading *The Glass Castle*.

Robert J. Smith's *Ancestor Worship in Contemporary Japan* reports:

> I can detect nothing in ordinary usage [of the term *hotoke*] today that reflects anything other than the serene assumption that the dead of the family are all buddhas.

In *Empty Words* Garfield argues that, upon Madhyamaka analysis, "the 'I' as a future tense subject in the Bodhisattva resolution is gratuitous." The bodhisattva is one who commits to bringing about awakening for the sake of all beings. It makes no sense to consider this awakening "mine." Garfield therefore defends (against significant criticism) the position that when one understands emptiness, the bodhisattva aspiration does not require commitment to belief in traditional notions of rebirth.

The concluding lines I adapted from Shantideva's *Guide to the Bodhisattva's Way of Life* (*Bodhisattva-carya-avatara*).

About the Author

Guy Newland is a professor of religion and chair of the Department of Philosophy and Religion at Central Michigan University, where he has taught since 1988. He has authored, edited, and translated several books on Tibetan Buddhism, including the three-volume translation of *The Great Treatise on the Stages of the Path to Enlightenment* and *Introduction to Emptiness*. Since the loss of his wife Valerie Stephens in 2013, he has expanded his teachings, given to universities and Dharma centers, to include topics on death, dying, and grief.

Also Available from Wisdom Publications

Zen Encounters with Loneliness
Terrance Keenan

"Every few years, if you're lucky, a book comes along that changes your life. *Zen Encounters with Loneliness* is one of those books."—Satya Robyn, author of *Afterwards*

A Heart Full of Peace
Joseph Goldstein
Foreword by His Holiness the Dalai Lama

"In this short but substantive volume, Joseph Goldstein, who lectures and leads retreats around the world, presents his thoughts on the practice of compassion, love, kindness, restraint, a skillful mind, and a peaceful heart as an antidote to the materialism of our age."—*Spirituality & Practice*

If You're Lucky, Your Heart Will Break
Field Notes from a Zen Life
James Ishmael Ford

"A valuable companion filled with encouragement for beginners and experienced meditators alike."—Diane Eshin Rizzetto, author of *Waking Up to What You Do*

About Wisdom Publications

Wisdom Publications is the leading publisher of classic and contemporary Buddhist books and practical works on mindfulness. To learn more about us or to explore our other books, please visit our website at wisdompubs.org or contact us at the address below.

Wisdom Publications
199 Elm Street
Somerville, MA 02144 USA

We are a 501(c)(3) organization, and donations in support of our mission are tax deductible.

Wisdom Publications is affiliated with the Foundation for the Preservation of the Mahayana Tradition (FPMT).

The Blue Poppy and the Mustard Seed
A Mother's Story of Loss and Hope
Kathleen Willis Morton

"This is an extraordinarily moving, beautiful, and compassionate book about the universal subject of loss and how one couple came to understand why the Buddha's request to bring him a mustard seed from any household where no one had ever died could never be fulfilled. Totally life-affirming."—*Mandala*

Bad Dog!
A Memoir of Love, Beauty, and Redemption in Dark Places
Lin Jensen

"It reads like something Steinbeck might have written had he been a Buddhist, and I can pay an author no higher compliment."—Christopher Moore, bestselling author of *A Dirty Job*